Gene A Smith
1-15-91

COLONIAL POPULATION

COLONIAL POPULATION

BY

ROBERT R. KUCZYNSKI

DEPARTMENT OF SOCIAL BIOLOGY
LONDON SCHOOL OF ECONOMICS

NEGRO UNIVERSITIES PRESS
NEW YORK

Originally published in 1937
by Humphrey Milford, London

Reprinted 1969 by
Negro Universities Press
A Division of Greenwood Publishing Corp.
New York

SBN 8371-1668-6

PRINTED IN UNITED STATES OF AMERICA

CONTENTS

INTRODUCTION

OFFICIAL data on the total population are available for every colony in the world. Some of the figures are fairly accurate while others may be wide of the mark. Telling the population of a country is like telling the age of a person. If you are asked to tell the age of a man whom you have never seen and of whom you merely know that he has written a history of the South African War, any figure you may suggest would be a wild guess. If, however, you learned that he served in that war and that he has a son in a public school, you would be in a position to make a reasoned guess since you would have good reason to assume that he is not under 55 and not over 75. If you then heard that his wife is older than he, you would have sufficient data on which to base an estimate. But in order to know his actual age you would have to ascertain the date of his birth.

The actual population of a country can be ascertained only through an enumeration of the people living at a given moment in that country. All figures obtained by other means than a genuine, all-inclusive census are estimates or guesses. Unfortunately, many population figures are published without a clear indication as to how they were arrived at. Quite often they are stated to be census results, although they are based in part on estimates or guesses. Where not even a partial census has been taken, the figures are always presented as estimates although in many cases they are at best reasoned guesses. For some countries for which the same figure is published year-in year-out it would be very difficult to trace its origin. People who have trusted one or another figure would shudder if they discovered how it was computed.[1] I must confine

[1] In the 1920's the population of Hong Kong was put at over a million. The only basis for this excessive 'estimate' was the fact that 'the amount of nightsoil now being collected approximates to 2,500 piculs or nearly four million taels, which, at taels 3 per head, gives a population of over 1,300,000, without allowing for wastage'. See *Report on the Census of the Colony of Hong Kong taken on the Night of March 7, 1931*, p. 28.

myself here briefly to characterizing the difference between population estimates and population guesses.

For some countries, such as Ethiopia, Liberia, Iran, and Peru, all population figures are wild guesses, and the same is true, for example, of most Spanish colonies where all data for a reasoned guess are lacking. The same conditions prevail in particular areas of many territories, for example, in the 'unpatrolled' regions of New Guinea. In other colonies where the population figures are based on such criteria as the number of huts or the number of natives paying a poll-tax we may speak of a reasoned guess. If, however, the authorities know not only the number of huts but have ascertained in addition for numerous villages in the various regions of the colony the average number of people per hut, or if they have ascertained for numerous villages in various regions of the colony the proportion of the inhabitants paying the poll-tax, they will be in a position to estimate the total population of the colony. They may even be able to make such an estimate if they have taken an actual census for, say, three-quarters of the area of the colony and have some idea of the density of the population in the rest of the colony. The proportion of the colonial population which actually has been enumerated varies greatly for the various parts of the world. In Africa it is only a very small fraction. Moreover, in many colonies where the population has been enumerated the last census was taken in 1921. The most recent figures published there are again either reasoned guesses or estimates.

While official data on the total population have been published for every colony, separate figures for males and females are often not available either because no attempt at all has been made to distinguish the sexes or because the population is subdivided merely into adult males, adult females, and children. There are, moreover, many cases where the number of adult males has been estimated on the basis of the known number of taxpayers while the figure given for the adult females is at best a reasoned guess. The figures for children in such cases are, as a rule, without any value, because they suffer from the additional defect that the term 'child' itself is extremely vague.

Some attempts, to be sure, have been made to classify the people by quinquennial or decennial age groups but they do not cover more than a negligible fraction of the total colonial population.[1]

For many colonies the population has been classified by race. But often the tables as published, while possibly satisfying the needs of the local administration, fail to show the facts which are of general interest and which would enable comparisons between the various colonies to be made. Every student of colonial problems would like to know the number of whites, the number of Asiatic non-natives (East Indians, Chinese, Japanese), and the number of natives, and for the American colonies in addition the number of negroes. But many colonial reports which distinguish the population by race do not convey this information.

The data on country of birth and on nationality do not present the same ambiguity as the data on race, but, in many cases, are difficult to interpret if no conclusive data on races are given simultaneously. All other classifications, such as those by occupation, religion or literacy, are made for only very few colonies.

Birth and death registration is compulsory for Europeans nearly everywhere, but in many colonies, and especially in most populous colonies, is either not introduced for natives or at least not adequately enforced. Vital statistics of the colonial population, as a whole, are therefore in a most unsatisfactory state.

It may seem surprising to a reader who has studied many colonial reports that our knowledge of the colonial population of the world is characterized here as being utterly inadequate. He will be reluctant to trust my judgement, after having found it stated in nearly every census report that the accompanying statistics are more accurate than all previous figures; after having seen life tables computed

[1] In very many colonies not even the Europeans are classified according to sex and age. In the French Cameroons where they were subdivided formerly into adult males, adult females, and children, recent statistics distinguish merely between 'heads of families' on the one hand and 'women and children' on the other hand. The heads of families include numerous females. Persons who belong to neither group, such as soldiers, apparently have been counted in some years as *chefs de famille*, in other years as women or children.

for native populations, percentages of pregnancies resulting in abortions, still-births, and live-births such as have never been ascertained for any European country, or figures showing the differential fertility of monogamous and of polygamous households; and after having read plausible explanations of any slight change in the number of inhabitants (a decrease being attributed, as a rule, to emigration, a moderate increase to sanitary measures, and an excessive increase to closer enumeration).

In point of fact, censuses do not at all improve automatically. Since a permanent census staff exists in hardly any colony the quality of a colonial census depends mainly on the skill of the official directing the census, and on the funds put at his disposal. In most cases this official has had little census experience or none at all. We read in the report on the census taken on 5 May 1931 in Northern Rhodesia:

> The Census Office Staff consisted of the Director, one Lady Clerk and one (native) office boy. The Director assumed duty early in January, the Lady Clerk at the beginning of May.[1]
>
> Neither of the two European members of the staff have had previous experience of census duties. The results obtained are therefore the work of amateurs who have had at their disposal the 1921 Census Report of Northern Rhodesia and other Census Reports of neighbouring territories.[2]

Such a frank statement is very rare and we owe it in this case perhaps to the fact that the Director of Census was a man of remarkable ability who succeeded in preparing a very satisfactory report without having had any former experience. But as long as colonial census staffs consist of a Director without previous census experience, of a lady clerk equally inexperienced who assumes duty in the very week when the census is taken, and of a native office boy, not too much reliance should be placed on the contention that the census they have taken is far superior to any census taken previously.

Inasmuch as an improvement of the censuses depends on an increase of the funds granted for such purposes,

[1] Northern Rhodesia, *Report of the Director of Census regarding the Census taken on the 5th May, 1931*, p. 5.

[2] Ibid., p. 42.

the situation is most dispiriting. Many of the British colonial censuses due in 1931 have not been taken at all; they were considered as a luxury which one had to dispense with in a period of depression. Other censuses were very much curtailed. In Ceylon, for example, where comprehensive censuses had been taken every ten years from 1871 to 1921, 'a full Census was taken only in the Town of Colombo with a population of 287,729 out of a total population in the Island of 5,312,548; on the estates with a population of 790,376, particulars with regard to the total population, sex, and race were supplied by the Superintendents; in the rest of the Island, only the figures of the total population were collected.'[1] In other colonies, the sums allocated for census purposes are so small that it is not even possible to carry out a bare enumeration of the population. The 1936 census was by far the cheapest census ever taken in the Union of South Africa. It cost about £80,000, or 2d. per head. Not before the final report is available will it be possible to judge whether, and if so to what extent, the economies made affected the quality of the census work. But so much is certain, no one familiar with the task involved will consider the sum spent in 1936 as extravagant. Yet the last 'census' in Nigeria, with double the population of the Union, cost £5,000 or one-quarter of a farthing per head! This is not the place to discuss the financial capacity of the various colonies—*A* may say that Nigeria simply 'cannot afford' to spend more on a census than a quarter of a farthing per head, and *B* may answer that in Nigeria, with a *yearly* budget of £5,000,000, there cannot be any necessity of limiting the expenses for the *decennial* census to £5,000—my purpose is mainly to emphasize that in many colonies the grants for census purposes are utterly inadequate and that since 1921 conditions on the whole have not improved.

It is easy to understand that the lack of comparable censuses and of adequate birth and death registration has induced many colonial administrators and medical officers to try other means of ascertaining fertility and mortality.

[1] *Report on the Census of Ceylon, 1931*, p. iii.

One method which has gained much favour recently is to question native women about their pregnancies, the number of children they have borne, the number of deceased children, etc. It is conceivable that such investigations, in spite of the discouraging experiences associated with similar investigations in Europe, might lead to valuable results if they are made on a sufficiently large scale, if either the women are grouped by age or only women past the child-bearing age are questioned, and if the women understand the questions and are ready to answer them correctly. But as, usually, one or another of these conditions is not fulfilled, these sample surveys have contributed very little towards improving our knowledge of the fertility and mortality of colonial populations.

It is easy also to understand that the authors of colonial reports are tempted to draw far-reaching conclusions from the scanty population data at their disposal. But the extent to which many of them yield to this temptation is appalling. It thus has become almost a universal habit to use the ratio of children to adults as a gauge of fertility, mortality, or population growth. Although a brief glance at a few life tables shows that this ratio may be extremely low or extremely high in a stationary population it has become an axiom for most authors of colonial reports that a high ratio of children to adults is a proof that the population is increasing rapidly and that a low ratio is a proof of a declining population. Many of them believe furthermore that a high ratio of children to adults is a proof of a low child mortality, while it requires not more than a little common sense to realize that, other things being equal, a country with a high child mortality is bound to have a higher ratio of children to adults than a country with a low child mortality.

But what perhaps more than anything else prevents many people from perceiving how little we know of the colonial population is the fact that they find in most colonial reports plausible explanations of any increase or decrease in the official figures. Let us suppose the official infant mortality rate has decreased. Unless the registration of births and deaths is strictly enforced, which is very seldom the case, this decrease may be due either to an actual decrease of mortality, or to an improvement in birth registration, or to a deterioration in death registration, or to two or three of these events. In the majority of cases, it will be impossible for the official in charge of the vital statistics to know what has actually happened. But how rare are the reports where the impossibility is admitted! And since each of the explanations is plausible, the reader will accept the explanation given as the correct one. Let us assume that the official population figure has decreased. The head of the administration is very much surprised by this result. He has no reason to assume that the new census was less complete than the preceding one. He has not learned of any epidemic that could have reduced the population. The most innocuous explanation is emigration. Let us take a concrete example. The 1934 Report to the League of Nations on the British Cameroons says: 'In the Adamawa Districts the annual census . . . showed a total decrease in population of 5,405 or 2·5 per cent. The decrease is fairly evenly distributed over the various districts, and the fluctuation due to temporary migration is normal.' The reader thus learns not only that there was emigration but also that the decrease was fairly evenly distributed over the various districts and that the migration was temporary and normal. How could he fail to be impressed by such a profound knowledge of the population movements in the Adamawa Districts? He could fail only if he took the trouble of checking the figures. He would then discover that the decrease in the official population figure was due to an arithmetical error, that the census actually showed no decrease of 5,405, but an increase of 307, and that an explanation does not necessarily look less plausible if the event which is explained has not occurred.

All this may sound like destructive criticism. I wish it were. Because the problem is not how to improve the existing colonial statistics. The problem is rather how to convince the colonial offices that what is needed in most colonies is an absolutely new departure. The population statistics of most colonies are to-day in a condition similar, in many respects, to that of the population statistics of most European countries 150 years ago. The censuses taken in 1801 in England and France were not an improvement on the earlier statistics, they were a new departure. The difficulties to be overcome were tremendous, and the first censuses were by no means perfect. The difficulties to be overcome in such colonies as Nigeria, French West or French Equatorial Africa are also tremendous, and the first genuine censuses will likewise not be perfect. But our ignorance of the colonial population of the world will not be lessened essentially unless a fresh start is made.

The data contained in this little book are then of most unequal value. Some are as accurate as the census figures of the most advanced countries in the world. Others are not more trustworthy than the population figures of most European countries in the eighteenth century. I have confined myself, moreover, to summarizing the official statistics referring to the total population, its distribution by race and by continent of birth, and to giving, in addition, a brief description of the state of birth and death registration. I do not reproduce the actual number of births and deaths because the available data cover only a very limited number of colonies. For the same reason, no attention has been paid to the statistics of sex, age, occupation, religion or literacy.[1]

[1] The reader interested in the statistics of nationality should consult *World Statistics of Aliens* by Imre Ferenczi, a volume published recently by the International Labour Office.

CHAPTER I

TOTAL POPULATION

THE Economic Intelligence Service of the League of Nations publishes every year an estimate of the population for each country of the world. We summarize in Table I the figures for 31 December 1934, distinguishing between self-governing and non-self-governing (colonial and mandated) areas.[1]

Table I. Population of Self-Governing and of Non-Self-Governing Areas, 31 December 1934[2]

Continent	*Self-governing areas*	*Non-self-governing areas*	*Total*	*Non-self-governing per cent. of Total*
Africa	33,140,000	111,934,000	145,074,000	77·2
America ..	256,293,000	5,144,000	261,437,000	2·0
Asia	987,235,000	148,516,000	1,135,751,000	13·1
Europe ..	524,110,000	272,000	524,382,000	0·1
Oceania ..	8,260,000	2,020,000	10,280,000	19·6
Total ..	1,809,038,000	267,886,000	2,076,924,000	12·9

This estimate indicates that of a total world population of 2,080 millions, 270 millions, or 13 per cent. lived in colonial or mandated areas, and that 55 per cent. of these 270 millions lived in Asia, 42 per cent. in Africa, and 3 per cent. in other continents.

Table II shows the population of the colonial and mandated areas according to the administrating Powers.

1 There is no consensus of opinion as to which areas should be considered as 'self-governing' and which as 'non-self-governing'. We follow here on the whole the procedure of the League of Nations but exclude from the non-self-governing areas the 'self-governing colony' of Southern Rhodesia. For a brief discussion of the problems involved, see *Raw Materials and Colonies* (The Royal Institute of International Affairs, Information Department Papers, No. 18), p. 15.

2 See *Statistical Year-Book of the League of Nations, 1935-6*, pp. 19-24.

It appears that of the total of 270 millions, one-quarter live under British administration, one-quarter under Dutch administration, one-quarter under French administration, and one-quarter under the administration of another Power.

Table II. Population of Colonial and Mandated Areas, 31 December 1934

(In thousands)

DEPENDENCIES, PROTECTORATES, COLONIES, ETC.

Administrating Powers	*Africa*	*America*	*Asia*	*Europe*	*Oceania*	*Total*
Australia	—	—	—	—	281	281
Belgium	9,400	—	—	—	—	9,400
Denmark	—	17	—	—	—	17
France	37,000	540	22,850	—	100	60,490
Great Britain	35,930	2,546	12,390	271	358	51,495
Great Britain—Egypt ..	5,800	—	—	—	—	5,800
Great Britain—France ..	—	—	—	—	60	60
Italy	2,350	—	135	—	—	2,485
Japan	—	—	29,600	—	—	29,600
Netherlands	—	247	64,450	—	—	64,697
Newfoundland	—	4	—	—	—	4
New Zealand	—	—	—	—	16	16
Norway	—	—	—	1	—	1
Portugal	7,450	—	1,270	—	—	8,720
Spain	1,000	—	—	—	—	1,000
United States of America	—	1,790	13,055	—	410	15,255
Internat. Administration	80	—	—	—	—	80
Total	99,010	5,144	143,750	272	1,225	249,401

MANDATED TERRITORIES

Administrating Powers	*Africa*	*America*	*Asia*	*Europe*	*Oceania*	*Total*
Australia	—	—	—	—	670	670
Belgium	3,500	—	—	—	—	3,500
France	3,062	—	3,250	—	—	6,312
Great Britain	6,095	—	1,516	—	3	7,614
Japan	—	—	—	—	70	70
New Zealand	—	—	—	—	52	52
Union of South Africa ..	267	—	—	—	—	267
Total	12,924	—	4,766	—	795	18,485

Table III shows the population of each colonial and mandated area at the last census before 1932 and on 31 December 1931 to 1935.

Table III. Population of Colonial and Mandated Areas, Last Census (before 1932) and 31 December 1931-5

Area	Administration	Last Census before 1932 (1)	31 Dec. 1931 (2)	31 Dec. 1932 (3)	31 Dec. 1933 (4)	31 Dec. 1934 (5)	31 Dec. 1935 (6)
			AFRICA				
Algeria	French	6,553,451	6,650,000	6,700,000	6,850,000	7,030,000	7,234,684
Angola	Port.	2,615,000	2,700,000	2,700,000	2,700,000	2,700,000	...
Basutoland ..	Brit.	498,781	600,000	650,000	650,000	570,000	562,411
Bechuanaland ..	Brit.	152,983	160,000	160,000	160,000	170,000	265,756
Belgian Congo ..	Belg.	—	9,441,211	9,401,844	9,390,146	9,300,836	11,000,000
Cameroons ..	Brit. M.	797,312	774,863	781,865	781,115	778,668	817,970
Cameroons ..	Fr. M.	2,201,966	2,250,000	2,250,000	2,298,495	2,230,201	2,341,105
Cape Verde Islands ..	Port.	148,533	148,533	150,553	153,182	156,923	...
Eritrea	Ital.	600,573	630,000	600,000	600,000	620,000	...
French Equatorial Africa	French	3,196,969	3,200,000	3,200,000	3,323,629	3,435,000	3,386,000
French West Africa	French	14,575,973	14,675,000	14,486,587	14,404,142	14,468,828	14,702,583
Gambia	Brit.	199,520	200,000	200,000	208,094	210,000	197,811
Gold Coast ..	Brit.	2,869,854	2,950,000	2,965,000	3,045,201	3,120,000	3,230,550
Kenya	Brit.	—	3,040,940	3,076,343	3,084,752	3,094,279	3,084,351
Libya	Ital.	704,123	715,000	720,000	720,000	730,000	888,636
Madagascar ..	French	3,759,019	3,730,000	3,772,569	3,820,987	3,847,000	...
Mauritius ..	Brit.	402,897	400,800	398,337	401,007	404,190	407,020
Morocco ..	French	5,404,860	5,450,000	5,500,000	5,500,000	5,600,000	6,296,136
Morocco ..	Span.	—	750,000	717,029	720,273	795,202	...
Mozambique	Port.	3,995,831	4,000,000	4,000,000	4,050,000	4,150,000	4,100,000
Nigeria	Brit.	19,130,859	19,200,000	19,300,000	19,349,921	19,092,295	19,106,282
Northern Africa	Span.	113,630	100,000	115,000	115,000	115,000	...
Northern Rhodesia	Brit.	1,309,528	1,386,000	1,393,000	1,382,000	1,378,000	...
Nyasaland ..	Brit.	1,603,454	1,630,000	1,609,915	1,611,314	1,603,914	1,603,257
Port. Guinea ..	Port.	364,929	340,000	380,000	390,403	380,000	400,000
Réunion	French	197,933	200,000	200,000	200,000	200,000	209,000
Rio de Oro ..	Span.	—	22,000	20,000	20,000	20,000	...
Ruanda-Urundi ..	Belg. M.	—	3,451,501	3,451,450	3,036,597	3,293,170	3,387,180
St. Helena ..	Brit.	4,183	4,206	4,000	4,340	4,397	4,475
St. Thomé, etc.	Port.	59,060	60,000	60,000	60,000	60,000	...
Seychelles ..	Brit.	27,444	27,786	28,235	28,731	29,406	29,803
Sierra Leone ..	Brit.	1,768,631	1,790,000	1,800,000	1,800,000	1,800,000	1,890,000
Somali Coast ..	French	69,782	70,000	70,000	70,000	70,000	...
Somaliland ..	Brit.	—	347,385	347,385	347,385	347,391	347,383
Somaliland ..	Ital.	1,021,572	1,000,000	1,000,000	1,000,000	1,000,000	...
South West Africa	S.A.M.	227,739	270,487	274,290	273,333	266,930	359,516
Spanish Guinea ..	Span.	118,293	120,000	120,000	120,000	120,000	120,743
Sudan	Ang.-E.	—	5,687,835	5,507,925	5,728,551	5,816,376	5,767,818
Swaziland ..	Brit.	106,961	123,320	125,085	125,775	126,560	146,015
Tanganyika ..	Brit. M.	5,063,660	5,063,544	4,972,807	5,038,590	4,988,338	5,138,080
Tangier	Inter. A.	—	80,000	80,000	80,000	80,000	60,000
Togoland ..	Brit. M.	293,714	300,000	306,930	320,156	328,077	341,254
Togoland ..	Fr. M.	—	749,798	751,652	753,811	762,629	763,420
Tunis	French	2,410,692	2,450,000	2,500,000	2,500,000	2,530,000	2,603,385
Uganda	Brit.	3,553,534	3,553,534	3,584,758	3,620,193	3,640,636	3,661,099
Zanzibar ..	Brit.	235,428	245,842	235,307	237,374	244,104	234,261
			NORTH AMERICA				
Alaska	U.S.A.	59,278	59,800	60,200	60,600	61,000	61,500
Greenland ..	Dan.	16,901	17,046	17,000	18,163	17,000	18,000
Labrador ..	Newf.	3,774	4,264	4,000	4,411	4,451	4,716
St. Pierre, etc. ..	French	4,321	4,000	4,000	4,000	4,000	4,330

Area	*Administration*	*Last Census before 1932* (1)	*31 Dec. 1931* (2)	*31 Dec. 1932* (3)	*31 Dec. 1933* (4)	*31 Dec. 1934* (5)	*31 Dec. 1935* (6)
CENTRAL AMERICA							
Antigua	Brit.	29,767	31,235	32,144	32,424	33,060	33,700
Bahamas	Brit.	59,828	60,650	61,812	62,679	63,763	64,982
Barbados ..	Brit.	156,774	173,674	176,874	180,055	182,440	184,912
Bermuda	Brit.	29,173	29,136	29,819	30,339	31,028	31,190
British Honduras	Brit.	51,347	52,139	52,945	53,770	54,744	55,448
Cayman Islands	Brit.	5,253	6,182	6,000	6,188	6,209	6,156
Curaçao	Dutch	55,160	71,769	75,372	79,395	83,254	87,104
Dominica ..	Brit.	37,059	43,098	44,103	45,239	46,298	47,394
Grenada	Brit.	66,302	78,662	81,000	82,624	83,888	85,626
Guadeloupe ..	French	267,407	270,000	270,000	270,000	270,000	246,497
Jamaica ..	Brit.	858,118	1,050,667	1,073,493	1,090,269	1,104,775	1,121,823
Martinique ..	French	234,505	237,000	240,000	238,645	244,908	246,497
Montserrat ..	Brit.	12,120	12,350	12,880	13,062	13,161	13,264
Panama Canal Z.	U.S.A.	39,467	41,000	42,000	42,000	46,000	41,190
Puerto Rico ..	U.S.A.	1,543,913	1,583,700	1,615,400	1,647,000	1,678,600	1,723,534
St. Kitts, Nevis ..	Brit.	38,214	36,067	36,730	36,888	37,521	37,742
St. Lucia ..	Brit.	51,505	59,676	61,135	62,000	63,804	64,959
St. Vincent ..	Brit.	47,961	51,995	49,665	52,006	53,622	55,219
Trinidad	Brit.	412,783	414,572	419,559	425,572	432,058	439,994
Turks etc. Islands	Brit.	5,612	5,300	5,300	...	5,300	5,300
Virgin Islands ..	Brit.	5,082	5,040	5,209	5,360	5,488	6,100
Virgin Islands ..	U.S.A.	22,012	22,000	22,000	22,000	22,000	...
SOUTH AMERICA							
British Guiana	Brit.	318,312	313,619	317,813	321,260	323,171	328,219
Falkland Islands	Brit.	3,101	2,903	2,903	3,077	3,107	3,180
French Guiana ..	French	32,596	29,000	30,000	26,000	26,000	...
Surinam	Dutch	—	155,888	158,194	161,208	164,085	166,343
ASIA							
Aden, Perim ..	Brit.	51,478	51,000	51,000	51,000	51,000	...
Aegean Islands ..	Ital.	130,842	131,507	132,919	134,384	135,884	137,162
Brunei	Brit.	30,135	30,285	30,595	32,869	32,971	33,732
Ceylon	Brit.	5,312,548	5,367,153	5,427,039	5,463,211	5,637,000	5,617,000
Cyprus	Brit.	347,959	350,486	354,215	357,934	361,653	365,372
Federated Malay States	Brit.	1,713,519	1,670,879	1,610,000	1,620,000	1,703,591	1,813,714
Formosa	Jap.	4,592,537	4,803,976	4,932,433	5,060,507	5,194,980	5,212,719
French India ..	French	286,410	270,000	283,243	281,684	282,850	282,397
French Indo-China	French	21,451,486	21,600,000	21,900,000	22,300,000	22,300,000	23,030,355
Hong Kong ..	Brit.	849,751	878,947	900,796	922,643	944,492	966,341
Korea	Jap.	21,058,305	20,262,958	20,599,876	20,791,321	21,125,827	22,898,695
Kuria Muria Is. ..	Brit.	—	...	2,000	2,000	2,000	...
Kwang Chau Wan	French	206,270	250,000	250,000	250,000	250,000	...
Kwantung ..	Jap.	1,328,011	1,275,185	1,323,866	1,408,755	1,497,600	1,656,763
Macao	Port.	157,175	170,000	170,000	170,000	170,000	170,000
Maldive Islands ..	Brit.	79,281	...	80,000	80,000	80,000	...
Netherlands Indies	Dutch	60,727,233	61,900,000	62,560,000	63,500,000	64,450,000	...
North Borneo ..	Brit.	270,223	270,536	275,000	274,195	275,000	284,813
Palestine ..	Brit. M.	1,035,821	1,040 000	1,080,000	1,140,000	1,210,554	1,308,114
Philippines ..	U.S.A.	10,314,310	12,419,100	12,589,400	12,758,400	12,927,400	13,096,400
Port. India ..	Port.	579,969	580,000	600,000	600,000	600,000	...
Saghalien ..	Jap.	295,196	287,377	293,172	300,298	313,130	331,949
Sarawak	Brit.	—	600,000	600,000	600,000	600,000	475,000
Socotra	Brit.	—	12,000	12.000	12,000	12,000	12,000
Straits Settlements	Brit.	1,125,779	1,085,301	1,060,000	1,040,710	1,090,000	1,143,792
Syria, Lebanon	Fr. M.	—	2,800,000	·3,000,000	3,200,000	3,130,054	3,267,000
Timor	Port.	474,363	480,000	480,000	500,000	500,000	460,655
Trans-Jordan ..	Brit. M.	—	270,000	305,000	305,000	305,000	331,600
Unfed. Malay St.	Brit.	1,527,167	1,489,543	1,510,000	1,512,662	1,600,000	1,620,125
EUROPE							
Gibraltar ..	Brit.	21,372	16,908	16,609	16,397	15,847	16,865
Malta	Brit.	258,400	244,002	248,062	251,832	255,185	256,140
Spitzbergen ..	Norw.	550	600	600	600	1,000	2,500

Area	*Administration*	*Last Census before 1932* (1)	*31 Dec. 1931* (2)	*31 Dec. 1932* (3)	*31 Dec. 1933* (4)	*31 Dec. 1934* (5)	*31 Dec. 1935* (6)
			OCEANIA				
American Samoa	U.S.A.	10,055	10,000	10,000	10,561	10,000	11,557
Brit. Solomon Is.	Brit.	94,066	95,000	95,000	95,000	95,000	...
Caroline, etc., Is. . .	Jap. M.	69,626	73,027	78,457	82,252	90,651	102,238
Cook Islands . .	N.Z.	13,863	15,204	15,440	15,697	15,891	16,443
Fiji Islands . .	Brit.	157,266	185,573	189,398	193,238	197,449	198,379
French Settlements	French	39,713	40,000	40,000	40,000	40,000	...
Gilbert, Ellice Is. . .	Brit.	33,474	33,416	33,685	34,085	34,337	33,809
Guam	U.S.A.	18,509	20,000	19,673	20,000	20,391	20,899
Hawaii	U.S.A.	368,336	377,859	380,000	380,000	380,000	384,437
Nauru	Brit. M.	2,066	2,692	2,316	2,641	2,677	2,696
New Caledonia . .	French	57,165	57,000	57,000	60,000	60,000	53,245
New Guinea . .	A.M.	—	552,000	551,000	671,000	671,000	672,000
New Hebrides . .	Ang.-F.	—	60,000	60,000	60,000	60,000	...
Norfolk	Austr.	717	992	1,074	1,231	1,198	1,161
Papua	Austr.	—	280,000	280,000	280,000	280,000	300,000
Tokelau Islands . .	N.Z.	1,033	1,048	...	1,147	1,179	1,198
Tonga	Brit.	28,839	29,439	29,454	30,693	31,589	33,332
Western Samoa . .	N.Z. M.	40,229	45,918	46,840	48,859	53,087	54,363

In order rightly to appraise the figures in Tables I, II, and III, it should be remembered, first of all, that for many areas the population has never been actually enumerated. According to the *Statistical Year-Book of the League of Nations* no census of the total population has yet been taken in the following colonial and mandated areas :[1]

Africa. Belgian Congo, Morocco (Spanish), Mozambique, Rio de Oro, Ruanda-Urundi, Somaliland (British), Sudan, Tangier, Togoland (French).

America. Surinam.

Asia. Kuria Muria Islands, Sarawak, Socotra, Syria and Lebanon, Trans-Jordan.

Oceania. New Guinea, New Hebrides, Papua.

The people living in these territories constitute probably 10 or 12 per cent. of the total population of the colonial and mandated areas. But even this list is not quite complete. The Year-Book mentions a census of the total population of Kenya, 7 March 1931 ; but the Annual Colonial Report for Kenya Colony and Protectorate, 1935, states : 'No accurate census of the native population has yet been made. The population figures are based on estimates made by the administrative authorities, and are

[1] See *Statistical Year-Book of the League of Nations*, *1935-6*, pp. 19-27. Many self-governing areas, such as Afghanistan, Arabia, China, Ecuador, Ethiopia, Iran, Iraq, Liberia, and Nepal, have likewise never taken a census.

related to the number of male adult taxpayers in the various districts.' There are, moreover, many colonies and mandated areas for which the authorities claim to have taken a 'census' while the figures were actually arrived at by estimates based, as in Kenya, on the enumeration of a section of the population.

Unfortunately the censuses of some of the most populous colonies are particularly incomplete. The 1931 census of Nigeria (including the British Cameroons) showed the population to be 19,928,171. But the Government Statistician, in his analysis of the results, estimated the actual population at 22,000,000, and added: 'This estimate is more likely to err in defect than in excess.'[1] The census figures of the adjoining colonies of French West and Equatorial Africa are certainly not more trustworthy than those of Nigeria, and the same is true of some other important colonial and mandated areas. As to the estimates for the territories where a census has never been taken, they come for certain colonies, such as the Belgian Congo (where they are based on thorough partial enumerations), probably as near the truth as some of the so-called censuses. For other territories they are at best reasoned guesses, which may be easily off the mark by 20 or more per cent.

But even where adequate censuses have been taken, the results in many cases are not strictly comparable. The data frequently do not refer to the *de facto* population, but to the *de jure* population. Owing to the considerable migration of labourers, especially between various African colonies, the *de jure* population may easily exceed or lag behind the *de facto* population by as much as 10 per cent. The comparability of the numbers of Europeans, in particular, is hampered by the fact that some censuses exclude the military and the shipping population while others include them.[2]

It should be realized, furthermore, that even where an

[1] *Census of Nigeria, 1931*, vol. I, p. 23.

[2] The problem involved in the inclusion or exclusion of the military and shipping has been ably discussed in the *Report on the Census of Ceylon, 1921* (vol. I, part I, p. 233): 'It has hitherto been the practice, in connexion with the Census of Ceylon, to regard as the standard definition of the population that which excludes the military and shipping, chiefly on the ground that they are fluctuating and uncertain elements, which have less claims to

adequate census has been taken this may have been a long time ago.[1] Where no adequate records of the changes in the population since the census are available, the official population estimates for post-censal years are frequently made on the assumption that the population will have increased in the same arithmetical or geometrical progression as it did between the last two preceding censuses. It is evident that such estimates are rather uncertain but few people probably will be aware how far actually the figures thus obtained may be off the mark, even if the lapse of time since the last census is short. It may suffice to mention as a proof the official estimates for Johore. According to the census of 1 April 1931, the population numbered 505,311. 'The population estimated by geometrical progression' at mid-year 1932, 1933, and 1934 was 545,320, 580,020, and 617,340 respectively.[2] By applying the same method, the result for mid-year 1935 would have been 657,000. Actually, however, as

---

inclusion than the others. It is true that most of the shipping population is accidentally in Ceylon waters at the time of the Census, and, in no other sense can be said to be part of the population of Ceylon . . . The difficulty is that, if we begin to draw distinctions as to the parts of the *de facto* population, which are, or are not, to be included in the definition of "population", we might well exclude ships' passengers who have landed for the night of the Census, tourists, traders on a short visit from India, and several others whose claims to inclusion are as slender as those of the shipping population . . .

The inclusion of the 'military population' is advisable also because the meaning of the term varies greatly in different areas. See *Report on the Census of Ceylon, 1931*, vol. I, p. 1 : 'It is to be noted that "Military", in general, includes persons enumerated by Military enumerators, and may exclude units counted by the civil staff. It may also include Volunteers, and soldiers' families and servants.'

Unfortunately the question of the inclusion or exclusion of the Military and Shipping is sometimes dealt with rather carelessly. The *Statistical Abstract for the British Empire, 1926 to 1935*, pp. 3-4, thus contains the following foot-notes referring to the most recent censuses :

Gibraltar, Malta, St. Helena, Ceylon. 'The population is exclusive of the military and persons on ships in harbours.'

Cyprus, Bermuda. 'The population is exclusive of the military.'

Sierra Leone. 'Exclusive of persons on ships.'

Straits Settlements. 'The military and the floating population are included in the population figures.'

As a matter of fact the figures for St. Helena and Cyprus do include the military. The figure for Straits Settlements includes neither the persons enumerated on the railway nor the population on sea-going ships. The figures for Mauritius and Hong Kong do not include the military. The figure for Barbados does not include the persons on ships.

[1] For some self-governing countries of South America the last census was taken more than twenty years ago (Argentine, 1914; Uruguay, 1908; Bolivia, 1900; Paraguay, 1899; Peru, 1876).

[2] See *Colonial Reports Annual*, No. 1635, p. 5; 1671, p. 5; 1708, p. 5.

stated in the Report for 1935,[1] the population had fallen rapidly in 1931-3 'owing to an exodus of the migrant population . . . and it was probably not until about the end of 1934 that the population rose again to about the level of the census figure. In these circumstances, the method of estimation by geometrical progression adopted as the basis of previous reports is clearly unsatisfactory . . . It has therefore been decided to change the basis . . . and adopt . . . estimates obtained by adding to the census population figures the excess of births over deaths since the census and a proportion of the migrational surplus for Malaya as a whole as given in the Malaya Migration Statistics.' The 1935 mid-year population thus estimated was 528,219.[2]

While the method of obtaining post-censal figures by adding to the census population the excess of births over deaths and the excess of arrivals over departures is theoretically perfect, its practical value depends on the completeness of registration. Experience, however, shows that while births, deaths, and arrivals may be registered adequately, the registration of departures is usually incomplete. As a consequence thereof, population figures computed by this method are likely to be too high.

Whereas all the figures in Tables I and II are computed from data contained in the *Statistical Year-Book of the League of Nations*, most of the figures entered in Table III are taken from official reports for the various colonial

[1] See *Colonial Reports Annual*, No. 1756, p. 5.

[2] Estimates based on the population growth in prior intercensal periods are, of course, particularly risky if the last census was taken a long time ago. As an example we may confront the official estimates as of 31 December 1935 for some South African areas with the results of the Censuses of 5 May 1936:

Area	*Census 3 May 1921*	*Estimate 31 Dec. 1935*	*Census 5 May 1936*
Union of South Africa	6,928,580	8,658,000	9,588,665
Basutoland	498,781	650,000	562,411
Bechuanaland	152,983	160,000	265,756
Swaziland	112,951	127,355	146,015

The estimates for the Union of South Africa, Basutoland, and Swaziland are taken from *Statistical Abstract for the British Empire, 1926 to 1935*, p. 3, for Bechuanaland from League of Nations, *Annual Epidemiological Report, 1935*, p. 65.

and mandated areas. Whenever possible, we have shown the *de facto* population (including Military and Shipping). Details about our sources and brief comments on the data are given in the Appendix. At this place we want merely to warn the reader against drawing conclusions from an apparent trend in the population figures. Where the same figure appears for every year this is usually due to the fact that the authorities, very wisely, refrained from making a new guess. Where the figures increase or decease this will in many cases be due to actual changes in the population but will in other cases be due either to a new enumeration or to changes in the methods of estimating the population.

Chapter II

POPULATION BY RACE

Most census reports of colonial and mandated areas contain some data on race. But few of the figures for the different territories are comparable. The reasons for the chaotic state of these statistics are manifold. We shall confine ourselves to stating the two most important :

1. Wherever there is a social inequality among several races, more or less numerous members of the less favoured races succeed in being allocated to that race which is considered as the superior one. This, of course, is a problem with which not only the colonial censuses are confronted. In the United States of America, although the colour line is drawn there probably more sharply than in any other country of the world, 'many individuals of mixed blood whose Negro characteristics are not physically prominent are without doubt classified as white'.[1]

In the British Dominions and Colonies, the figures of 'pure whites' are swelled much more than in the United States by the erroneous allocation of persons of mixed blood. The report on the 1921 census in the Union of South Africa states 'that coloured persons on the borderline of race, particularly in parts of the Cape Province, were enumerated in 1911 on their own statement as Europeans. In 1921 the necessary corrections were effected by enumerators, whose local knowledge was of special value in this matter.'[2] The 'Instructions to Supervisors' indicate how these corrections were made :

It will often occur that an Enumerator, especially in the poorer localities, will be asked for, say, a European form (C.1) by persons who obviously cannot be classed as white. In such cases Enumerators must be instructed to refrain from giving offence by any comment

[1] Leon E. Truesdell, Chief Statistician for Population, Bureau of the Census, 'Value of the Population Census for Research', *The Annals* (Philadelphia), November 1936, p. 331.

[2] *Census of the Population of the Union of South Africa, Enumerated 3rd May, 1921, Report*, p. 36.

or question in the presence of the parties concerned, but to make a private note on the completed forms against the names of any persons he considers cannot be classed as European, and report the circumstances to you. Thereafter the particulars in respect of the persons in question should be transferred to the form or forms applicable to their race.[1]

When, in spite of these precautions, the 1921 census revealed for 1911-21 an increase of only 3·7 per cent. for the 'Coloured' as against 19·1 per cent. for the Whites, the Director of Census stated: 'These people through physical degeneration appear to lack the necessary stamina to withstand diseases affecting the respiratory organs, and fall an easy prey to the pneumonic form of influenza.'[2] In subsequent years the 'Coloured', according to an estimate published in 1936[3], were supposed to have increased from 545,548 on 3 May 1921 to 612,000 on 30 June 1935, or by 12·2 per cent., but the census of 5 May 1936 showed the 'Coloured' to number 767,984, or 40·8 per cent. more than on 3 May 1921. It is safe to conclude therefrom that a considerable proportion of Coloured were enumerated as Whites in 1921.

The report on the 1931 census of Sierra Leone complains that 'a considerable number of Colony-born natives insist on calling themselves "Creoles", either through false pride or ignorance'.[4]

The author of the Report on the last census of Grenada, in the section on the race composition of the population, tells of similar experiences:[5]

I would preface this section of the report with the same comment as that of the Compiler of the 1881 Census, to wit 'many persons of mixed blood have improperly and ridiculously returned themselves as "white."' This statement applies with equal force to the present enumeration: the 'Whites' therefore may safely be reduced by about 10 per cent. and the 'Mixed' correspondingly increased. The figures are dealt with as returned. While the schedules were

[1] *Census of the Population of the Union of South Africa, Enumerated 3rd May, 1921 Report*, p. 10.

[2] Ibid., p. 39.

[3] See *Official Year Book of the Union of South Africa, 1934-5*, p. 909.

[4] Sierra Leone, *Report of Census for the Year 1931*, p. 47.

[5] *Report and General Abstracts of the Census of 1921*, p. 10.

being examined one could not help noticing that persons undoubtedly of mixed blood seemed to have undergone an albescent re-incarnation. The ridiculous aspect is evidenced by the fact that of the issue of the same parents of mixed blood, one was returned as White while another was entered Mixed.

An ingenious method of segregating self-styled Europeans from pure Europeans is applied in the returns for British Guiana. The reports distinguish there between (1) Europeans (other than Portuguese), (2) Europeans (Portuguese), and (3) Mixed. Translated from the official language into plain English the three groups evidently mean : (1) Persons of pure European descent, (2) Portuguese half-castes of European habits, (3) other half-castes.

The difficulty that Portuguese and other non-British half-castes of European descent with European habits consider themselves as Europeans is also encountered in some British Colonies in Asia. The report on the 1931 Census of British Malaya states :[1]

> Of the 2,376 non-British Europeans, 825 were returned as 'Dutch', but it is probable that many of these should have been included under Eurasians, the same being true in the case of the 117 'Portuguese'. As to the Dutch, it must be borne in mind that, in the Netherlands Indies, whence comes the great majority of these people, the distinction between European and Eurasian is not maintained as we maintain it, and, for census and other administrative purposes, the two classes are grouped together as 'Europeans and those assimilated with them' or 'Europeans' simply. It is therefore only to be expected that many Eurasians originating from the Dutch possessions should describe themselves as Europeans, Hollanders or 'Dutch'. . . . the French [contingent] has decreased from 332 to 331 ; it must however be recognized that these latter figures probably include a number of Indians and Eurasians from French India.[2]

The nearest approach to the practice observed by the Continental Powers of Europe is to be found in the colonial

[1] British Malaya, *Report on the 1931 Census and on certain Problems of Vital Statistics*, pp. 74-5.

[2] See also the *Report on the Census of Ceylon, 1921* (vol. I, part I, p. 214 ; vol. IV, p. 33): 'The Dutch and Portuguese include a certain number of persons of mixed descent, whose claim to the nationality marked might have proved doubtful if inquiries—which were not made as being too inquisitorial—had been carried out.'

and mandated areas of New Zealand. In the Census returns of Cook Islands and Niue the 'Europeans' include all persons with at least one-half European blood; in Western Samoa they include all persons with more than one-half European blood.

2. The incomparability due to differences in the meaning of the original data is enhanced very much by differences in the presentation of the data. The ideal solution evidently would be to make the same fundamental distinctions for all areas and to add for each separate area those special distinctions which are best apt to characterize the race composition of its population. This method has been applied to the French colonies and mandated territories. The fundamental distinctions there are: (1) Europeans and Assimilated, (2) Natives. The results have been summarized by continents as follows:[1]

Continent	*Europeans and Assimilated*	*Natives*
Africa	1,655,000	37,454,000
Asia	80,000	24,411,000
America	535,000	1,000
Oceania	40,000	117,000
Total	2,310,000	61,983,000

The results for some individual colonies read as follows:

Colonies	*Europeans and Assimilated*	*Natives*
French Equatorial Africa ..	4,687	3,192,000
New Caledonia	15,795	41,000
Algeria	881,584	5,588,000
Somali Coast	1,362	68,000
French West Africa	89,900	14,486,000
French Settlements (Oceania) ..	23,055	17,000
Réunion	192,961	5,000
Guadeloupe and Dependencies	267,407	—
Martinique	234,505	—

[1] See Statistique générale de la France, *Résultats statistiques du recensement général de la population effectué le 8 mars 1931*, vol. I, part I, p. 113.

Unfortunately, however, the terms 'Europeans and Assimilated' and 'Natives' do not have the same meaning for the various colonies.

The 4,687 Europeans and Assimilated in French Equatorial Africa comprise only persons of European descent. The 15,795 Europeans and Assimilated in New Caledonia comprise only persons of European descent; the 41,000 'Natives' are composed of 29,000 Natives and 12,000 Asiatics.

The 881,584 Europeans and Assimilated in Algeria include 98,646 Algerian Jews, all naturalized natives and their descendants, and all non-Moslem foreigners. The 1,362 Europeans and Assimilated in Somali Coast include 734 'Hindus, Abyssinians, and Jews'.

The 89,900 Europeans and Assimilated in French West Africa include 68,812 native French citizens. The 23,055 Europeans and Assimilated in the French Settlements in Oceania include 16,998 Oceanian French citizens.

The 192,961 Europeans and Assimilated in Réunion include the total population except 5,000 Arabs, Kaffirs, Chinese, Indians, and Madagascans who are entered as natives.

The Europeans and Assimilated in Guadeloupe and Dependencies (267,407) and in Martinique (234,505) include the total population of those islands.

The figures for the Europeans and Assimilated are then not comparable because, while they sometimes comprise only persons of European descent, they sometimes comprise all non-natives (including Asiatics), sometimes persons of European descent and natives with French citizenship, sometimes all persons of European descent and all descendants of imported negro slaves (thus excluding practically only Asiatics), and sometimes the total population.

The figures for the natives, on the other hand, are not comparable because, while they sometimes comprise all natives and nobody else, they sometimes exclude natives with French citizenship, sometimes comprise all natives (Africans or Oceanians) and all Asiatics, and sometimes only foreign elements who are neither the descendants of Europeans nor of imported slaves.

The French attempt to observe uniform fundamental distinctions by races for census purposes has thus failed completely. The British authorities, for over a hundred years, have made a similar effort by means of the Blue Books which contain uniform schedules in which the census results should be entered. But most colonial administrations do not conform to these rules and make returns which do not correspond to the headings of the columns. All that has been achieved so far is that in some cases some neighbouring colonies have voluntarily agreed on a uniform classification. The variety, therefore, is enormous, and we shall confine ourselves to presenting the various types of classification used in Africa.[1]

I. Basutoland, Bechuanaland, Northern Rhodesia, and Swaziland:[2]

1. Europeans: persons of pure European descent (whether born in Europe or not).

2. Asiatics: persons born of, or descended from, races belonging to the continent of Asia (including Syrians and Parsees).

3. Coloured: pure blooded persons other than Europeans, Asiatics, and Bantus, and all half-castes (includes, amongst others, Hottentots, Bushmen, Cape Malays, Creoles, Negroes, and Cape Coloured).

4. Natives: pure blooded aboriginals of the Bantu race.

II. Kenya, Tanganyika, Uganda, Zanzibar:

1. Europeans.

2. East Indians and Arabs: (*a*) Indians, (*b*) Goans, (*c*) Arabs.

3. Others: other non-natives.[3]

4. Natives.

[1] We shall omit the classification of the natives by tribes.

[2] These colonies have adopted the classification in use in the Union of South Africa. See *Census of the Union of South Africa, 1921, Report*, pp. 10, 26. The same classification is applied also in South West Africa.

[3] Kenya and Tanganyika subdivide the 'Others' further into (*a*) Coloured, (*b*) Half-castes, (*c*) Others. The 'Coloured in Kenya include Seychellois, Mauritians, and Ceylonese.

III. Sierra Leone:

1. Europeans.

2. Asiatics: (*a*) Syrians, (*b*) Indians, (*c*) Arabs, (*d*) Asiatic Greeks.

3. Non-native Africans: (*a*) Sierra Leoneans ('Liberated Africans and their descendants'), (*b*) West Indians, (*c*) Mulattos (European-African, Syrian-African, Indian-African, European-Asiatic), (*d*) Other non-Native Africans (Liberians, American Negroes, and Africans from other colonies).

4. Natives: Members of African native tribes.

IV. British Somaliland:

1. Whites: Europeans and other white population.

2. East Indians: (*a*) Natives of British India, (*b*) Natives of Portuguese India.

3. Coloured: (*a*) Arabs, (*b*) Persians, (*c*) Turkish, (*d*) Egyptians.

4. Black: (*a*) Abyssinians, (*b*) Sudanese, (*c*) Natives of Nyasaland, (*d*) Swahilis.

5. Natives: Somali.

V. Nigeria, British Cameroons, Nyasaland:

1. White races: 'Europeans, Americans, and persons of European or American extraction.'

2. Asiatics.

3. Natives.

VI. Gambia, Gold Coast, British Togoland:

1. Non-Africans.

2. Africans.

VII. Mauritius:

1. Europeans: 'persons born in Europe, of European parents, or born in Mauritius of European parents.'

2. Mauritians: 'persons of whatever origin [except European] who have become permanently settled in

Mauritius and who are following European customs and religions.'

3. Indians : 'members of the population following the customs and religions of India.'

4. Chinese.

VIII. Seychelles :

1. Europeans and persons of European descent and Africans.

2. Asiatics : (*a*) Indians, (*b*) Chinese.

Table IV shows the race composition of the population of those colonial and mandated areas, for which useful figures are available.[1] In Africa, America, Asia, and Europe we have distinguished Whites (persons of pure European descent), Asiatics (persons of Asiatic descent including half-castes), and Africans (persons of African descent including half-castes) ; in Oceania we have distinguished Whites, Asiatics, Half-castes, and Natives.[2]

Table IV. Population of Colonial and Mandated Areas by Race

Area		*Date*	*Whites*	*Asiatics*	*Africans*	*Others, Unknown*	*Total*
				A. AFRICA			
Algeria ..	.. (7)	8 Mar. 1931	801,086	5,752,365		—	6,553,451
	(8)	June 1934	829,489	6,081,055		—	6,910,544
	(9)	8 Mar. 1936	858,909	6,375,775		—	7,234,684
Basutoland	.. (7)	3 May 1921	1,603	172	497,006	—	498,781
	(8)	5 May 1936	1,434	341	560,636	—	562,411
Bechuanaland	.. (7)	3 May 1921	1,743	52	151,188	—	152,983
	(8)	5 May 1936	1,899	66	263,791	—	265,756
Belgian Congo	.. (7)	1 Jan. 1932	22,290	139	9,418,750	32	9,441,211
	(8)	1 Jan. 1933	18,539	127	9,383,146	32	9,401,844

[1] Details about our sources and brief comments on the data are given in the Appendix.

[2] The group 'Others, Unknown' comprises—apart from persons for whom the race was not stated—for example, the Red Indians in Alaska, British Guiana, and Surinam, the Eskimoes in Greenland, the non-native Pacific Islanders and the Negroes in the various colonial and mandated areas of Oceania.

Area	*Date*	*Whites*	*Asiatics*	*Africans*	*Others, Unknown*	*Total*
Cameroons .. (7)	31 Dec. 1931	278	—	774,585	—	774,863
(Brit. M.) (8)	31 Dec. 1932	254	—	781,611	—	781,865
(9)	31 Dec. 1933	304	—	780,811	—	781,115
(10)	31 Dec. 1934	316	—	778,352	—	778,668
(11)	31 Dec. 1935	354	—	817,616	—	817,970
Cameroons .. (7)	1 July 1931	2,134	30	2,199,802	—	2,201,966
(Fr. M.) (8)	31 Dec. 1933	1,999	39	2,296,457	—	2,298,495
(9)	31 Dec. 1934	2,047	59	2,228,095	—	2,230,201
(10)	31 Dec. 1935	2,257	67	2,338,781	—	2,341,105
Cape Verde Islands (7)	31 Dec. 1933	864	—	152,318	—	153,182
French Equatorial Africa .. .. (7)	8 Mar. 1931	4,463	22	3,192,410	74	3,196,969
French West Africa (7)	1 July 1931	16,078	5,010	14,554,885	—	14,575,973
(8)	31 Dec. 1932	21,564	5,722	14,459,301	—	14,486,587
(9)	31 Dec. 1933	21,466	5,865	14,376,811	—	14,404,142
(10)	31 Dec. 1934	19,403	5,316	14,444,109	—	14,468,828
(11)	8 Mar. 1936	19,061	5,737	14,677,785	—	14,702,583
Gambia .. .. (7)	24 April 1931	217	57	199,246	—	199,520
Gold Coast .. (7)	26 April 1931	2,509	630	2,866,715	—	2,869,854
Kenya .. .. (7)	6 Mar. 1931	16,812	56,930	2,967,198	—	3,040,940
(8)	31 Dec. 1932	17,249	51,245	3,007,849	—	3,076,343
(9)	31 Dec. 1933	17,332	50,094	3,017,326	—	3,084,752
(10)	31 Dec. 1934	17,501	51,593	3,025,185	—	3,094,279
(11)	31 Dec. 1935	17,997	53,718	3,012,636	—	3,084,351
Madagascar .. (7)	1 July 1931	19,620	10,475	3,730,406	—	3,760,501
(8)	31 Dec. 1932	21,213	9,646	3,741,710	—	3,772,569
(9)	31 Dec. 1933	21,954	10,121	3,788,912	—	3,820,987
Mauritius .. .. (7)	26 April 1931	645	300,000	102,252	—	402,897
Morocco (French) (7)	8 Mar. 1931	177,831	233	5,226,796	—	5,404,860
(8)	8 Mar. 1936	194,696	—	6,101,440	—	6,296,136
Nigeria .. .. (7)	23 April 1931	4,672	490	19,125,697	—	19,130,859
Northern Rhodesia (7)	5 May 1931	13,846	176	1,295,506	—	1,309,528
Nyasaland .. (7)	26 April 1931	1,975	1,591	1,599,888	—	1,603,454
(8)	31 Dec. 1932	1,901	1,583	1,606,431	—	1,609,915
(9)	31 Dec. 1933	1,817	1,474	1,608,023	—	1,611,314
(10)	31 Dec. 1934	1,800	1,401	1,600,713	—	1,603,914
(11)	31 Dec. 1935	1,781	1,400	1,600,076	—	1,603,257
Port. Guinea .. (7)	1931	983	26	363,920	—	364,929
Ruanda Urundi .. (7)	31 Dec. 1931	904	550	3,450,047	—	3,451,501
(8)	31 Dec. 1932	811	513	3,450,126	—	3,451,450
(9)	31 Dec. 1933	803	559	3,035,235	—	3,036,597
(10)	31 Dec. 1934	868	534	3,291,768	—	3,293,170
(11)	31 Dec. 1935	893	580	3,385,707	—	3,387,180
Sierra Leone .. (7)	26 April 1931	718	1,216	1,766,697	—	1,768,631
Somali Coast .. (7)	1 Jan. 1931	628	499	68,655	—	69,782
Somaliland (Brit.) (7)	26 April 1931	68	2,157	345,158	—	347,383
South West Africa (7)	3 May 1921	19,432	11	208,296	—	227,739
(8)	1931	32,840	—	237,647	—	270,487
(9)	1932	32,000	—	242,290	—	274,290
(10)	1933	31,600	—	241,733	—	273,333
(11)	1934	31,600	—	235,330	—	266,930
(12)	1935	31,800	—	248,264	—	280,064
(13)	5 May 1936	31,049	—	328,467	—	359,516

Area		Date	Whites	Asiatics	Africans	Others, Unknown	Total
Swaziland ..	(7)	3 May 1921	2,205	7	104,749	—	106,961
	(8)	31 Dec. 1931	2,650	10	120,660	—	123,320
	(9)	31 Dec. 1932	2,725	10	122,350	—	125,085
	(10)	31 Dec. 1933	2,775	10	122,990	—	125,775
	(11)	31 Dec. 1934	2,830	10	123,720	—	126,560
	(12)	31 Dec. 1935	2,885	10	124,460	—	127,355
	(13)	5 May 1936	2,735	2	143,278	—	146,015
Tanganyika ..	(7)	26 April 1931	8,228	32,584	5,022,848	—	5,063,660
	(8)	31 Dec. 1931	8,217	32,687	5,022,640	—	5,063,544
	(9)	31 Dec. 1932	8,151	31,477	4,933,179	—	4,972,807
	(10)	31 Dec. 1933	8,304	30,126	5,000,160	—	5,038,590
	(11)	31 Dec. 1934	8,193	29,640	4,950,505	—	4,988,338
	(12)	31 Dec. 1935	8,455	33,447	5,096,178	—	5,138,080
Togoland (Brit. M.)	(7)	26 April 1931	43	—	293,671	—	293,714
Togoland (Fr. M.)	(7)	1931	588	58	749,152	—	749,798
	(8)	1932	585	72	750,995	—	751,652
	(9)	1933	448	63	753,300	—	753,811
	(10)	1934	418	55	762,156	—	762,629
	(11)	1935	418	55	762,947	—	763,420
Tunis	(7)	22 Mar. 1931	175,764	2,234,928 (Asiatics and Africans)		—	2,410,692
Uganda	(7)	28 May 1931	2,001	14,665	3,536,868	—	3,553,534
	(8)	31 Dec. 1932	1,811	14,061	3,568,886	—	3,584,758
	(9)	31 Dec 1933	1,854	14,204	3,604,135	—	3,620,193
	(10)	31 Dec. 1934	1,959	15,086	3,623,591	—	3,640,636
	(11)	31 Dec. 1935	1,994	14,860	3,644,245	—	3,661,099
Zanzibar	(7)	28 Mar. 1931	278	37,513	197,637	—	235,428

B. AMERICA

North America

Area		Date	Whites	Asiatics	Africans	Others, Unknown	Total
Alaska	(7)	1 Oct. 1929	28,640	479	136	30,023	59,278
Greenland ..	(7)	1 Oct. 1930	413	—	—	16,488	16,901
	(8)	1 Jan. 1934	334	—	—	17,829	18,163
St. Pierre, Miquelon	(7)	1 July 1931	4,321	—	—	—	4,321

Central America

Area		Date	Whites	Asiatics	Africans	Others, Unknown	Total
Antigua	(7)	24 April 1921	914	18	28,835	—	29,767
Barbados ..	(7)	24 April 1921	10,748	—	146,026	—	156,774
Bermuda	(7)	17 May 1931	12,706	—	16,467	—	29,173
	(8)	31 Dec. 1931	12,462	—	16,674	—	29,136
	(9)	31 Dec. 1932	12,756	—	17,063	—	29,819
	(10)	31 Dec. 1933	12,894	—	17,445	—	30,339
	(11)	31 Dec. 1934	13,167	—	17,861	—	31,028
	(12)	31 Dec. 1935	13,008	—	18,182	—	31,190
Cayman Islands ..	(7)	25 April 1921	1,994	—	3,259	—	5,253
	(8)	7 Aug. 1934	2,368	2	3,637	2	6,009
Dominica	(7)	24 April 1921	556	—	36,362	141	37,059
Grenada	(7)	24 April 1921	814	2,692	62,796	—	66,302
Jamaica	(7)	25 April 1921	14,476	22,306	817,643	3,693	858,118
Montserrat ..	(7)	24 April 1921	112	—	12,008	—	12,120
	(8)	31 Dec. 1932	101	—	12,779	—	12,880
	(9)	31 Dec. 1933	103	—	12,959	—	13,062
	(10)	31 Dec. 1934	105	—	13,056	—	13,161
	(11)	31 Dec. 1935	107	—	13,157	—	13,264
Panama Canal Z...	(7)	1 April 1930	18,814	244	20,385	24	39,467
Puerto Rico ..	(7)	1 April 1930	1,146,719	36	397,156	2	1,543,913
St. Kitts, Nevis ..	(7)	24 April 1921	1,219	36	36,959	—	38,214

Area		Date	Whites	Asiatics	Africans	Others, Unknown	Total
St. Vincent ..	(7)	26 April 1931	2,173	653	44,549	586	47,961
Trinidad, Tobago	(7)	26 April 1931	41,118	144,149	227,516	—	412,783
Turks & Caicos Is.	(7)	25 April 1921	210	—	5,402	—	5,612
	(8)	31 Dec. 1934	160	—	5,140	—	5,300
Virgin Islands ..	(7)	25 April 1921	36	—	5,046	—	5,082
(Brit.)	(8)	31 Dec. 1932	22	—	5,187	—	5,209
Virgin Is. (U.S.A.)	(7)	1 April 1930	2,010	40	19,962	—	22,012

South America

Area		Date	Whites	Asiatics	Africans	Others, Unknown	Total
British Guiana ..	(7)	26 April 1931	2,127	133,491	166,615	8,700	310,933
	(8)	31 Dec. 1931	2,085	134,938	167,883	8,713	313,619
	(9)	31 Dec. 1932	2,078	137,074	169,890	8,771	317,813
	(10)	31 Dec. 1933	2,051	138,223	172,096	8,890	321,260
	(11)	31 Dec. 1934	2,039	139,103	173,125	8,904	323,171
	(12)	31 Dec. 1935	2,186	141,575	175,414	9,044	328,219
Surinam	(7)	31 Dec. 1931	1,725	70,103	17,242	66,818	155,888
	(8)	31 Dec. 1932	1,798	71,584	17,000	67,812	158,194
	(9)	31 Dec. 1933	1,858	73,264	17,000	69,086	161,208
	(10)	31 Dec. 1934	1,886	74,967	17,000	70,232	164,085
	(11)	31 Dec. 1935	1,938	76,239	17,000	71,166	166,343

C. ASIA

Area		Date	Whites	Asiatics	Africans	Others, Unknown	Total
Brunei	(7)	1 April 1931	60	30,071	—	4	30,135
Ceylon	(7)	18 Mar. 1921	8,937	4,495,312	300	—	4,504,549
	(8)	26 Feb. 1931	9,153	5,297,418	300	—	5,306,871
	(9)	1 July 1932	9,700	5,376,100	300	—	5,386,100
	(10)	1 July 1933	9,800	5,405,400	300	—	5,415,500
	(11)	1 July 1934	10,000	5,541,300	300	—	5,551,600
	(12)	1 July 1935	10,100	5,588,100	300	—	5,598,500
Fed. Malay States	(7)	1 April 1931	6,350	1,706,680	4	62	1,713,096
Formosa	(7)	31 Dec. 1933	207	5,060,300	—	—	5,060,507
	(8)	31 Dec. 1934	219	5,194,761	—	—	5,194,980
French India ..	(7)	1 July 1931	740	283,636	—	—	284,376
French Indo-China	(7)	1 July 1931	31,114	21,420,372	—	—	21,451,486
	(8)	8 Mar. 1936	31,695	22,998,660	—	—	23,030,355
Hong Kong ..	(7)	7 Mar. 1931	16,476	833,227	32	16	849,751
Kwang Chau Wan	(7)	1 July 1926	270	206,000	—	—	206,270
Maldive Islands ..	(7)	18 Mar. 1921	—	70,413	—	—	70,413
Netherlands Indies	(7)	7 Oct. 1930	177,449	60,548,275	—	1,509	60,727,233
North Borneo ..	(7)	26 April 1931	362	269,856	2	3	270,223
Palestine	(7)	18 Nov. 1931	174,610	861,211		—	1,035,821
	(8)	30 June 1933	209,207	895,677		—	1,104,884
	(9)	30 June 1934	253,700	917,458		—	1,171,158
	(10)	31 Dec. 1934	282,970	927,584		—	1,210,554
	(11)	31 Dec. 1935	355,142	952,972		—	1,308,114
	(12)	31 Dec. 1936	384,045	982,659		—	1,366,704
Straits Settlements	(7)	1 April 1931	10,003	1,103,805	7	200	1,114,015
Timor	(7)	1931	625	473,586	152	—	474,363
Unfed. Malay States	(7)	1 April 1931	1,295	1,525,055	3	251	1,526,604

D. EUROPE

Area		Date	Whites	Asiatics	Africans	Others, Unknown	Total
Gibraltar	(7)	26 April 1931	17,494	57	62	—	17,613

Area	*Date*	*Whites*	*Asiatics*	*Half-castes*	*Natives*	*Others, Unknown*	*Total*
			E. OCEANIA				
American Samoa .. (7)	1 April 1930	227	11	877	8,926	14	10,055
Brit. Solomon Islands (7)	April 1931	478	172	—	93,415	1	94,066
Caroline, etc., Islands (7)	1 Oct. 1930	71	19,860	—	49,695	—	69,626
(8)	1 Oct. 1931	81	22,908	—	50,038	—	73,027
(9)	1 April 1932	82	25,782	—	50,045	—	75,909
(10)	1 Oct. 1932	82	28,306	—	50,069	—	78,457
(11)	1 April 1933	83	30,687	—	50,114	—	80,884
(12)	1 Oct. 1933	87	32,230	—	49,935	—	82,252
(13)	1 April 1934	86	35,345	—	50,174	—	85,605
(14)	1 Oct. 1934	83	40,232	—	50,336	—	90,651
(15)	1 April 1935	81	47,428	—	51,056	—	98,565
(16)	1 Oct. 1935	77	51,621	—	50,540	—	102,238
Fiji Islands .. (7)	24 April 1921	3,878	61,630	2,781	86,710	2,267	157,266
(8)	31 Dec. 1931	5,058	78,163	3,446	95,821	3,085	185,573
(9)	31 Dec. 1932	4,863	80,435	3,548	97,433	3,119	189,398
(10)	31 Dec. 1933	4,804	82,467	3,661	99,177	3,129	193,238
(11)	31 Dec. 1934	4,763	84,775	3,717	100,977	3,217	197,449
(12)	31 Dec. 1935	4,938	87,378	3,846	102,514	3,376	202,052
(13)	26 April 1936	4,028	86,821	4,574	99,267	3,689	198,379
French Settlements (7)	1 July 1931	5,882	4,423	—	28,324	1,084	39,713
Gilbert, Ellice Is. .. (7)	1931	249	728	231	32,164	—	33,372
(8)	30 June 1931	275	439	235	32,458	9	33,416
(9)	30 June 1932	251	398	—	33,036	—	33,685
(10)	31 Dec. 1933	244	396	—	33,445	—	34,085
(11)	31 Dec. 1934	238	360	—	33,739	—	34,337
(12)	31 Dec. 1935	280	536	—	32,993	—	33,809
Guam .. .. (7)	1 April 1930	1,205	865	—	16,402	37	18,509
Hawaii .. .. (7)	1 April 1930	73,702	236,323	28,224	22,636	7,451	368,336
(8)	30 June 1931	71,442	243,703	30,003	22,391	7,672	375,211
(9)	31 Dec. 1931	72,404	244,648	30,759	22,310	7,738	377,859
(10)	30 June 1932	73,365	245,592	31,515	22,230	7,805	380,507
(11)	30 June 1934	76,391	238,351	34,419	21,796	7,991	378,948
(12)	30 June 1935	81,075	237,572	35,978	21,710	8,122	384,457
(13)	30 June 1936	88,193	237,613	37,608	21,594	8,269	393,277
Nauru .. .. (7)	1 April 1931	147	1,105	—	1,426	14	2,692
(8)	1 April 1932	141	696	—	1,475	4	2,316
(9)	30 June 1933	165	936	—	1,527	13	2,641
(10)	1 April 1934	163	933	—	1,567	14	2,677
(11)	1 April 1935	158	931	—	1,603	4	2,696
(12)	1 April 1936	179	1,092	—	1,647	4	2,922
New Caledonia .. (7)	1 July 1931	15,848	12,631	—	28,502	184	57,165
(8)	1 July 1936	16,515	7,930	—	28,800	—	53,245
New Guinea.. .. (7)	4 April 1921	1,288	1,602	69	...	214	...
(8)	30 June 1933	3,191	1,651	195	...	179	...
New Hebrides .. (7)	1931	1,083	3,451	—	...	—	...
(8)	1932	1,068	1,925	—	...	—	...
(9)	1933	1,019	1,299	—	...	—	...
(10)	1934	979	1,322	—	...	—	...
(11)	1935	953	949	—	...	—	...
Norfolk .. .. (7)	4 April 1921	713	—	4	—	—	717
(8)	30 June 1933	1,230	—	1	—	—	1,231
Papua .. .. (7)	4 April 1921	1,343	136	158	...	441	...
(8)	30 June 1933	1,148	130	227	...	668	...
Tokelau Islands .. (7)	Feb. 1926	—	—	25	1,008	—	1,033
Tonga .. .. (7)	27 April 1931	482	—	265	27,700	392	28,839
(8)	27 April 1932	412	—	397	28,381	264	29,454
(9)	27 April 1933	409	—	436	29,620	228	30,693
(10)	27 April 1934	378	—	475	30,482	254	31,589
(11)	27 April 1935	434	—	352	30,724	363	31,873

In Table V we have made an attempt to show for every colonial and mandated area the number of Whites (persons of pure European descent). Table VI summarizes the figures for Whites by continents and by administrating Powers. It appears that the Whites, numbering about 4,500,000, constitute 1⅔ per cent. of the total population of the colonial and mandated areas. But over 3,500,000 of these Whites live in territories bordering the Mediterranean or in Puerto Rico. In all other areas combined with a total population of about 250,000,000 there are hardly 1,000,000 Whites.

Table V. Whites in Colonial and Mandated Areas about 1935

Area	Date	Whites
AFRICA		
Algeria	8 Mar. 1936	858,909
Angola	31 Dec. 1935	30,000
Basutoland ..	5 May 1936	1,434
Bechuanaland ..	5 May 1936	1,899
Belgian Congo ..	1 Jan. 1936	18,500
Cameroons (Brit. M.)	31 Dec. 1935	354
Cameroons (Fr. M.)	31 Dec. 1935	2,257
Cape Verde Islands	31 Dec. 1933	864
Eritrea	21 April 1931	4,000
Fr. Equatorial Africa	8 Mar. 1931	4,463
French West Africa	8 Mar. 1936	19,061
Gambia	24 April 1931	217
Gold Coast ..	31 Dec. 1935	2,800
Kenya	31 Dec. 1935	17,997
Libya	21 April 1931	45,000
Madagascar ..	31 Dec. 1933	21,954
Mauritius	31 Dec. 1935	700
Morocco (French)	8 Mar. 1936	194,696
Morocco (Spanish)	1934	45,000
Mozambique ..	31 Dec. 1935	10,000
Nigeria	31 Dec. 1935	5,246
Northern Africa ..	31 Dec. 1935	90,000
Northern Rhodesia	31 Dec. 1935	9,913
Nyasaland ..	31 Dec. 1935	1,781
Port. Guinea ..	31 Dec. 1935	500
Réunion	31 Dec. 1935	70,000
Rio de Oro ..	31 Dec. 1930	297
Ruanda-Urundi ..	31 Dec. 1935	893
St. Helena	31 Dec. 1935	400
St. Thomé, etc. ..	31 Dec. 1935	500
Seychelles	31 Dec. 1935	500
Sierra Leone ..	26 April 1931	718
Somali Coast ..	1 Jan. 1931	628
Somaliland (Brit.) ..	26 April 1931	68
Somaliland (Ital.)	21 April 1931	1,500
South West Africa	5 May 1936	31,049
Spanish Guinea ..	31 Dec. 1935	1,500
Sudan	31 Dec. 1935	6,776
Swaziland	5 May 1936	2,735
Tanganyika ..	31 Dec. 1935	8,455
Tangier	31 Dec. 1935	12,000
Togoland (Brit. M.)	26 April 1931	43
Togoland (Fr. M.) ..	1935	418
Tunis	12 Mar. 1936	191,885
Uganda	31 Dec. 1935	1,994
Zanzibar	31 Dec. 1935	300

Area	Date	Whites
NORTH AMERICA		
Alaska	1 Oct. 1929	28,640
Greenland	Jan. 1934	334
Labrador	31 Dec. 1935	4,000
St. Pierre, etc. ..	1 July 1931	4,321
CENTRAL AMERICA		
Antigua	31 Dec. 1935	1,000
Bahamas	31 Dec. 1935	10,400
Barbados	31 Dec. 1935	13,000
Bermuda	31 Dec. 1935	13,008
British Honduras ..	31 Dec. 1935	1,100
Cayman Islands ..	31 Dec. 1935	600
Curaçao	31 Dec. 1935	3,500
Dominica	31 Dec. 1935	700
Grenada	31 Dec. 1935	1,050
Guadeloupe ..	31 Dec. 1935	21,600
Jamaica	31 Dec. 1935	19,000
Martinique	31 Dec. 1935	10,500
Montserrat	31 Dec. 1935	107
Panama Canal Zone	31 Dec. 1935	20,000
Puerto Rico ..	1 Dec. 1935	1,280,000
St. Kitts, Nevis ..	31 Dec. 1935	1,200
St. Lucia	31 Dec. 1935	1,000
St. Vincent ..	31 Dec. 1935	2,500
Trinidad	31 Dec. 1935	44,000
Turks, etc., Islands	31 Dec. 1934	160
Virgin Islands (Brit.)	31 Dec. 1932	22
Virgin Is. (U.S.A.)	31 Dec. 1935	2,000
SOUTH AMERICA		
British Guiana ..	31 Dec. 1935	2,186
Falkland Islands ..	31 Dec. 1935	3,180
French Guiana ..	31 Dec. 1934	25,000
Surinam	31 Dec. 1935	1,938
ASIA		
Aden, Perim ..	26 Feb. 1931	1,700
Aegean Islands ..	21 April 1931	10,000
Brunei	31 Dec. 1935	84
Ceylon	1 July 1935	10,100
Cyprus	31 Dec. 1935	250,000

Area	Date	Whites
Fed. Malay States	1 April 1931	6,350
Formosa	31 Dec. 1934	219
French India ..	1 July 1931	740
French Indo-China	8 Mar. 1936	31,695
Hong Kong ..	7 Mar. 1931	16,476
Korea	31 Dec. 1935	1,500
Kuria Muria Islands	31 Dec. 1935	—
Kwang Chau Wan	1 July 1926	270
Kwantung ..	31 Dec. 1935	50
Macao	31 Dec. 1935	2,000
Maldive Islands ..	18 Mar. 1921	—
Netherlands Indies	7 Oct. 1930	177,449
North Borneo ..	26 April 1931	362
Palestine	31 Dec. 1935	355,142
Philippines ..	31 Dec. 1935	50,000
Port. India	31 Dec. 1935	1,000
Saghalien	31 Dec. 1934	227
Sarawak	31 Dec. 1935	390
Socotra	31 Dec. 1935	50
Straits Settlements	31 Dec. 1935	12,100
Syria, Lebanon ..	31 Dec. 1935	5,000
Timor	31 Dec. 1935	500
Trans-Jordan ..	31 Dec. 1935	2,000
Unfed. Malay States	1 April 1931	1,295

Area	Date	Whites
EUROPE		
Gibraltar	26 April 1931	17,494
Malta	31 Dec. 1935	250,000
Spitzbergen ..	31 Dec. 1935	2,500
OCEANIA		
American Samoa ..	1 April 1930	227
British Solomon Is.	April 1931	478
Caroline, etc., Is. ..	1 Oct. 1935	77
Cook Islands ..	31 Dec. 1935	100
Fiji Islands ..	26 April 1936	4,028
French Settlements	1 July 1931	5,882
Gilbert, Ellice Is...	31 Dec. 1935	280
Guam	1 April 1930	1,205
Hawaii	30 June 1936	88,193
Nauru	1 April 1936	179
New Caledonia ..	1 July 1936	16,515
New Guinea ..	30 June 1935	4,176
New Hebrides ..	1935	953
Norfolk	30 June 1933	1,230
Papua	30 June 1933	1,148
Tokelau Islands ..	Aug. 1935	—
Tonga	April 1935	434
Western Samoa ..	31 Dec. 1935	400

Table VI. Whites in Colonial and Mandated Areas according to Administrating Powers about 1935

DEPENDENCIES, PROTECTORATES, COLONIES, ETC.

Administrating Powers	*Africa*	*America*	*Asia*	*Europe*	*Oceania*	*Total*
Australia	—	—	—	—	2,378	2,378
Belgium	18,500	—	—	—	—	18,500
Denmark	—	334	—	—	—	334
France	1,361,596	61,421	32,705	—	22,397	1,478,119
Great Britain	48,702	114,213	298,907	267,494	5,220	734,536
Great Britain—Egypt ..	6,776	—	—	—	—	6,776
Great Britain—France ..	—	—	—	—	953	953
Italy	50,500	—	10,000	—	—	60,500
Japan	—	—	1,996	—	—	1,996
Netherlands	—	5,438	177,449	—	—	182,887
Newfoundland	—	4,000	—	—	—	4,000
New Zealand	—	—	—	—	100	100
Norway	—	—	—	2,500	—	2,500
Portugal	41,864	—	3,500	—	—	45,364
Spain	136,797	—	—	—	—	136,797
United States of America	—	1,330,640	50,000	—	89,625	1,470,265
Internal Administration ..	12,000	—	—	—	—	12,000
Total	1,676,735	1,516,046	574,557	269,994	120,673	4,158,005

MANDATED TERRITORIES

Administrating Powers	*Africa*	*America*	*Asia*	*Europe*	*Oceania*	*Total*
Australia	—	—	—	—	4,176	4,176
Belgium	893	—	—	—	—	893
France	2,675	—	5,000	—	—	7,675
Great Britain	8,852	—	357,142	—	179	366,173
Japan	—	—	—	—	77	77
New Zealand	—	—	—	—	400	400
Union of South Africa ..	31,049	—	—	—	—	31,049
Total	43,469	—	362,142	—	4,832	410,443

Chapter III

POPULATION BY CONTINENT OF BIRTH

The country of birth has been ascertained at many colonial censuses, and for a fairly large number of areas the data have been published with details sufficient to permit a classification by continent of birth. Table VII shows the results for those colonial and mandated areas for which such figures are available. It is of particular interest to note that in many cases the majority of East Indians were born in the colony. Some outstanding examples are Mauritius, Trinidad, and the Fiji Islands. Of the 268,649 Indians enumerated in Mauritius (1931), only 6,835 were born in Asia. Of the 138,667 Indians enumerated in Trinidad and Tobago (1931), as many as 114,946 were born in Trinidad. Of the 85,002 Indians enumerated in the Fiji Islands (1936), 60,857 were born in the Colony. The proportion of Whites born in the Colony is very large all along the Mediterranean coast. The other African areas show great divergencies. Of the Whites in Basutoland (1921) two-thirds were born in Africa; of the Whites in Northern Rhodesia (1931) three-fifths. On the other hand, the proportion was only one-third in Kenya (1931), two-ninths in Tanganyika (1931), and one-sixth in Uganda (1931).

Table VII. Population of Colonial and Mandated Areas by Continent of Birth

Area		*Race*	*Europe*	*Africa*	*America*	*Asia*	*Oceania*	*At Sea, Unknown*	*Total*
				A. AFRICA					
Basutoland ..		Europeans ..	498	1,081	3	8	11	2	1,603
3 May 1921	(9)	Asiatics ..	—	88	1	83	—	—	172
		Coloured ..	—	1,068	—	1	—	—	1,069
Gambia									
24 April 1931	(8)	Colony, Total ..	196	13,892	10	57	—	215	14,370

Area	*Race*	*Europe*	*Africa*	*America*	*Asia*	*Oceania*	*At Sea, Unknown*	*Total*
Kenya .. 6 Mar. 1931 (12)	Europeans ..	9,647	5,713	340	685	355	72	16,812
	Indians ..	—	13,948	—	25,664	—	32	39,644
	Goans ..	—	937	—	3,027	—	15	3,979
	Arabs ..	—	7,409	—	4,743	—	14	12,166
	Other Non-natives	10	1,125	4	197	—	10	1,346
Mauritius .. 26 April 1931 (8)	General Pop. ..	391	115,068	12	47	15	133	115,666
	Indians ..	—	261,814	—	6,835	—	—	268,649
	Chinese ..	3	3,369	—	5,540	—	11	8,923
Northern Africa 31 Dec. 1930 (7)	Total ..	72,471	37,956	357	28	—	3,115	113,927
Northern Rhodesia 5 May 1931 (8)	Europeans ..	5,010	8,189	319	107	205	16	13,846
	Asiatics ..	—	43	—	133	—	—	176
	Coloured ..	—	405	3	1	—	16	425
Nyasaland .. 26 April 1931 (12)	Europeans ..	1,304	552	39	55	25	—	1,975
	Asiatics ..	—	110	—	1,470	—	11	1,591
Seychelles .. 26 April 1931 (7)	Europ., Africans	147	26,546	4	8	1	—	26,706
	Indians ..	1	159	—	343	—	—	503
	Chinese ..	—	43	—	192	—	—	235
Sierra Leone .. 26 April 1931 (8)	Europeans ..	571	13	53	9	5	—	651
	Asiatics ..	—	267	2	947	—	—	1,216
	Sierra Leoneans	1	35,886	3	—	—	2	35,892
	Other African Non-natives ..	3	1,028	70	5	—	42	1,148
South West Africa 3 May 1921 (14)	Europeans ..	6,270	12,931	45	26	44	116	19,432
Swaziland .. 3 May 1921 (14)	Europeans ..	270	1,914	13	1	7	—	2,205
	Asiatics,Coloured	—	445	1	5	—	—	451
Tanganyika .. 26 April 1931 (13)	Europeans ..	5,808	1,857	191	297	70	5	8,228
	Indians ..	2	9,545	—	13,873	—	2	23,422
	Goans ..	1	362	—	1,357	—	2	1,722
	Arabs ..	2	4,215	—	2,839	—	3	7,059
	Other Coloured ..	1	155	1	21	—	—	178
	Half-castes ..	—	29	—	1	—	—	30
	Other Non-natives	4	100	1	274	—	2	381
Tunis .. 22 Mar. 1931 (8)	Europeans ..	69,963	119,494	197	143	—	5,496	195,293
Uganda .. 28 May 1931 (12)	Europeans ..	1,497	314	71	94	20	5	2,001
	Indians ..	—	3,782	—	9,192	—	52	13,026
	Goans ..	—	263	—	856	—	5	1,124
	Arabs ..	—	189	—	326	—	—	515
	Others ..	—	553	2	45	—	1	601

B. AMERICA

Area	*Race*	*Europe*	*Africa*	*America*	*Asia*	*Oceania*	*At Sea, Unknown*	*Total*
Greenland 1 Oct. 1930 (9)	Europeans ..	352	—	56	—	—	—	408
Antigua 24 April 1921 (8)	Total	150	3	29,586	23	1	4	29,767
Bahamas 26 April 1931 (7)	Total	349	5	59,413	—	—	61	59,828
Barbados .. 24 April 1921 (8)	Total	620	26	156,007	17	2	102	156,774
	Excl. Shipping ..	388	24	155,779	17	2	102	156,312
British Honduras 26 April 1931 (7)	Total	306	7	50,784	185	13	52	51,347
Cayman Islands 25 April 1921 (9)	Total	8	—	5,202	—	—	43	5,253
Dominica 24 April 1921 (8)	Total	167	8	36,854	7	—	23	37,059

Area	Race	Europe	Africa	America	Asia	Oceania	At Sea, Unknown	Total
Grenada 24 April 1921 (8)	Total	119	41	65,937	199	1	5	66,302
Jamaica	East Indians	—	—	11,349	7,103	—	158	18,610
25 April 1921 (8)	Total	2,628	254	844,983	9,823	13	417	858,118
Montserrat 24 April 1921 (12)	Total	28	3	12,084	4	1	—	12,120
St. Kitts, Nevis 24 April 1921 (8)	Total	102	4	38,014	36	1	57	38,214
St. Lucia	East Indians	—	—	1,818	323	—	48	2,189
24 April 1921 (7)	Total	92	28	51,026	331	2	26	51,505
St. Vincent 26 April 1931 (8)	Total	68	4	47,837	25	—	27	47,961
Trinidad	East Indians	—	—	115,283	23,255	—	129	138,667
26 April 1931 (8)	Chinese	—	—	3,212	2,027	—	—	5,239
	Others	2,293	181	265,792	211	—	400	268,877
Virgin Islands	White	170	—	1,798	1	—	41	2,010
(U.S.A.)	Negro	2	—	17,227	—	—	14	17,243
1 April 1930 (8)	Mixed	11	—	2,695	2	—	11	2,719
	Other Coloured	—	—	27	9	—	4	40
British Guiana	Whites	1,069	—	1,058	—	—	—	2,127
26 April 1931 (13)	Half-castes	673	—	41,739	—	—	—	42,412
	Africans	—	67	124,136	—	—	—	124,203
	Asiatics	—	—	108,981	23,659	—	851	133,491
				C. ASIA				
Aden and Perim 26 Feb. 1931 (8)	Total	1,593	3,079	56	46,745	5	—	51,478
Brunei 1 April 1931 (8)	Europeans	44	—	8	8	—	—	60
Ceylon	Europeans	4,870	63	90	2,951	144	—	8,118
18 Mar. 1921 (13)	Eurasians	18	4	3	29,413	1	—	29,439
	Sinhalese, Tamils, Moors	15	42	1	4,421,117	2	—	4,421,177
	Malays	—	1	—	13,400	1	—	13,402
	Veddas	—	—	—	4,510	—	—	4,510
	Others	55	37	67	21,745	54	1	21,959
Cyprus 27 April 1931 (7)	Total	4,635	445	73	342,792	14	—	347,959
Fed. Malay States 1 April 1931 (8)	Europeans	4,278	—	135	1,343	592	2	6,350
Hong Kong	Chinese	122	18	780	820,104	398	7	821,429
7 Mar. 1931 (8)	Europeans	13,344	96	676	2,051	234	1	16,402
	Eurasians	10	7	38	764	18	—	837
	Local Portuguese	8	—	—	3,188	1	—	3,197
	Indians	1	3	4	4,736	—	1	4,745
	Japanese	2	—	3	2,199	1	—	2,205
	Others	2	12	71	843	8	—	936
Maldive Islands 18 Mar. 1921 (8)	Total	—	—	—	70,413	—	—	70,413
Palestine	Moslems	95	2,813	92	756,647	1	64	759,712
18 Nov. 1931 (13)	Jews	80,375	2,417	831	90,541	38	408	174,610
	Christians	7,850	911	920	81,653	42	22	91,398
	Others	330	10	11	9,749	—	1	10,101
Straits Settlements 1 April 1931 (8)	Europeans	7,227	—	246	2,093	417	20	10,003
Unfed. Malay States 1 April 1931 (8)	Europeans	946	—	8	260	81	—	1,295

Area	*Race*	*Europe*	*Africa*	*America*	*Asia*	*Oceania*	*At Sea, Unknown*	*Total*
		D. EUROPE						
Gibraltar 26 April 1931 (8)	Total	17,247	178	70	109	7	2	17,613
Malta 26 April 1931 (7)	Total	239,396	1,609	199	363	50	4	241,621
		E. OCEANIA						
American Samoa 1 April 1930 (8)	Whites	21	—	196	—	4	6	227
Cook Islands 20 April 1926 (7)	Non-natives ..	75	2	5	1	225	5	313
Fiji Islands 24 April 1921 (14)	Europeans ..	846	23	81	38	2,860	30	3,878
	Half-castes	1	—	1	2	2,663	114	2,781
	Indians ..	—	48	45	33,156	26,812	573	60,634
26 April 1936 (15)	Europeans ..	742	27	65	19	3,078	97	4,028
	Half-castes	—	—	1	—	4,571	2	4,574
	Indians	—	128	75	23,880	60,857	62	85,002
	Chinese	—	—	—	1,296	455	—	1,751
	Japanese ..	—	—	—	40	22	—	62
	Other Non-natives	—	—	1	3	5,302	5	5,311
Guam ..	Whites	45	—	1,060	4	81	15	1,205
1 April 1930 (8)	Filipinos	—	—	—	87	277	1	365
Hawaii 1 April 1930 (14)	Total	8,054	—	32,986	111,551	214,922	823	368,336
Nauru ..	Europeans ..	59	—	—	—	106	—	165
30 June 1933 (13)	Chinese	—	—	—	936	—	—	936
1 April 1934 (14)	Europeans ..	55	—	—	1	107	—	163
1 April 1935 (15)	Europeans ..	50	—	—	1	107	—	158
1 April 1936 (16)	Europeans ..	51	—	—	1	127	—	179
New Guinea 4 April 1921 (9)	Non-natives ..	686	8	14	1,457	941	67	3,173
30 June 1933 (10)	Non-natives	1,157	10	84	1,033	2,914	18	5,216
Norfolk 4 April 1921 (9)	Total	31	—	5	2	678	1	717
30 June 1933 (10)	Total	153	2	5	10	1,059	2	1,231
Papua 4 April 1921 (9)	Non-natives ..	487	7	27	50	1,498	9	2,078
30 June 1933 (10)	Non-natives ..	299	2	23	28	1,803	18	2,173
Western Samoa 1 Jan. 1926 (8)	Europeans ..	181	1	36	19	698	6	941

Chapter IV

BIRTH AND DEATH RECORDS

Birth and death registration is compulsory for Europeans in nearly every colonial and mandated area, and in many colonies vital statistics for Europeans are also published regularly. For non-Europeans, and particularly for natives, compulsory birth and death registration has not been introduced in many areas and there are few populous areas where it is adequately enforced. We shall give here a brief survey by continents, adding some comments for one area or another.

Africa

1. Compulsory birth and death registration has been introduced for the whole area of Algeria, Madagascar, Mauritius, Réunion, St. Helena, Seychelles, Tunis, Uganda, and Zanzibar.

Algeria. Registration for natives was made compulsory in 1882,[1] and vital statistics have been published from 1901 on.[2] The figures for both births and deaths in the Southern Territory are so low that the records in this section of the country appear to be utterly deficient. In the Northern Territory registration of male births may be fairly complete in many districts, but numerous female births are not registered, the sex ratio being about 120 male for 100 female registered births.[3] Deaths of infants evidently are recorded inadequately throughout the country. The gaps in the registration of deaths of older children and of adults are said to be greater for females than for males.[4]

[1] See H. Bunle, 'Notices statistiques sur la démographie des colonies françaises,' *Metron*, vol. IV, 1 June 1925, p. 627.

[2] See *Annuaire statistique de l'Algérie, 1934*, p. 93.

[3] In the Northern Territory, 99,687 male and 83,928 female native births were registered in 1934; see *Annuaire 1934*, p. 76. For the sex ratio in each of the years 1901 to 1930, see *Annuaire 1930*, pp. 70-3.

[4] See Henri Brenier, *Le problème de la population dans les colonies françaises*, pp. 27-30, Lyons, 1930; A. Laffont, *La mortinatalité et la mortalité infantile au point de vue pathologique, Afrique du Nord*, International Conference on African Children, No. 3, pp. 11-12, 17, Geneva, 1931; Julien Franc, 'La population de l'Algérie en 1931,' *Bulletin de la Société de Géographie d'Alger et de l'Afrique du Nord*, vol. XXXVII, 1932, pp. 157-8; 'Notes on Vital Statistics in Africa', League of Nations, *Epidemiological Report of the Health Section of the Secretariat, 1932*, pp. 121-2.

MADAGASCAR. According to Bunle (1925), the administration considered the registration of births and deaths to be complete.[1] But recent statistics indicate that in most districts birth registration is very deficient. Death registration, apart from the records of deceased infants, seems to be more satisfactory but is far from being complete throughout the country.[2]

MAURITIUS. Registration is compulsory and seems to be enforced.

RÉUNION. Registration was made compulsory for the whole population in 1848[3] and seems to be enforced.

ST. HELENA. Registration seems to be adequate.

SEYCHELLES. 'Registration of births, still-births and deaths is compulsory and these returns can be taken as correct.'[4]

TUNIS. Birth and death registration for the total population became compulsory on 1 January 1920.[5] According to Brenier (1930), registration for natives is as inadequate as in Algeria and is deficient even in Tunis and the other large towns.[6]

UGANDA. Registration was introduced in 1926. Births and deaths are registered by the chiefs. No returns are made from the Karamoja District (1931: 65,578 inhabitants). The official reports complain of faulty registration. There was a 'tendency to record births more accurately than deaths'.[7] But birth registration seems to have deteriorated in recent years; in the Western Province the birth rate decreased from 38·28 in 1929 to 25·05 in 1935.[8]

ZANZIBAR. 'It is probable that many births and deaths are unregistered.'[9] Registration of infant deaths is utterly deficient.

[1] See Bunle, p. 666.

[2] It may suffice to mention that in the Region of Tuléar with over 300,000 native inhabitants only 2,185 native births and 2,467 native deaths were registered in 1933.

[3] See Bunle, p. 663.

[4] Colony of Seychelles, *Annual Report of the Medical and Health Department for the year 1935*, p. 7.

[5] See Bunle, p. 644.

[6] See Brenier, p. 31. See also Laffont, pp. 20-21; 'Notes on Vital Statistics in Africa,' pp. 122-4.

[7] *Colonial Reports Annual*, 1645, *Uganda Protectorate, 1932*, p. 9.

[8] See Uganda Protectorate, *Annual Report of the Medical Department, 1935*, p. 28.

[9] Zanzibar Protectorate, *Blue Book, 1935*, p. 86.

The 1931-5 infant mortality rates computed by relating the number of deaths under one to the number of births were 78·2, 77·6, 61·2, 90·7, and 84·2, while the actual rate has been estimated officially at 200 to 400.[1]

2. Compulsory birth and death registration has been introduced for natives in some districts of the French Cameroons, French West Africa, Gambia, Gold Coast, Spanish Morocco, Nigeria, Northern Rhodesia, Sierra Leone, South West Africa, Anglo-Egyptian Sudan, and British Togoland.

CAMEROONS (French Mandate). Compulsory registration was introduced in 1930 in a large number of towns and villages. By the end of 1935 there were 309 registration offices scattered over 33 of the existing 47 Sub-divisions, but the official reports contain no data as to the population covered by those offices. 'Outside of the large centres the civil registration functions in a still imperfect manner.'[2]

FRENCH WEST AFRICA. Compulsory registration has been introduced in some towns, comprising about 2 per cent. of the total population, but it is doubtful whether registration even there is complete.[3]

GAMBIA. Compulsory registration has been introduced in the town of Bathurst (Island of St. Mary) with 14,000 inhabitants (7 per cent. of the total population). 'Vital statistics are recorded in the Island of St. Mary only, as, owing to the illiteracy of the people, the collection of reliable data in the Protectorate is impossible. . . . whereas all deaths taking place in Bathurst are registered (certificates of deaths and burials permits being required in all cases), in some instances births of infants, in particular to illiterate parents, are not reported.'[4]

[1] See *Colonial Report*, 1706, *Zanzibar Protectorate, 1934*, p. 7: 'It is believed that the correct rate is between three and four hundred per thousand births'; see also Ibid., 1766, *Zanzibar Protectorate, 1935*, p. 6: 'It is believed that the correct rate is over two hundred per 1000 births.'

[2] *Rapport annuel au Conseil de la Société des Nations sur l'administration sous mandat du territoire du Cameroun, 1935*, p. 155.

[3] See Mary Blacklock, *Still-birth and Infant Mortality from the pathological point of view, West Africa*, International Conference on African Children, No. 1, p. 7, Geneva, 1931; 'Notes on Vital Statistics in Africa,' pp. 130-2; Cazanove, *Essai de démographie des colonies françaises*, Bulletin de l'Office International d'Hygiène publique, Supplement to vol. XXII, No. 8, August 1930, pp. 11-21.

[4] *Colonial Report*, 1755, *The Gambia, 1935*, p. 12.

GOLD COAST, TOGOLAND (British Mandate). 'Birth and death registration is applied to 35 centres the total population of which equals some nine per centum of the population of the Gold Coast as a whole.'[1] 'The registration areas consist of townships and their immediate surroundings—that is the area contained within the town boundaries of the respective centres. . . . It is considered that among the better educated classes the value of birth registration is becoming yearly more apparent. In all centres, however, were it not for the constant vigilance of officers of the Health Branch of the Medical Department many births would not be registered. . . . When the Health Branch staff is busily engaged on epidemic disease prevention it is not uncommon to find a corresponding fall in the number of births registered in the affected centres.'[2] The extremely low death rates for some centres seem to indicate that death registration also is not complete.

SPANISH MOROCCO. Registration is apparently compulsory in the town of Ceuta,[3] comprising something like 5 per cent. of the total population of the Colony.

NIGERIA. 'The registration of vital statistics has been in existence in Lagos since 1867, and has during the present century reached a very fair standard of accuracy.'[4] 'Compulsory registration is also in force at Port Harcourt, Calabar and Kano Township but the figures are not yet sufficiently reliable for publication.'[5] The registration area comprises about 1 per cent. of the total population.

NORTHERN RHODESIA. Registration is compulsory in '411 villages with a population of 42,768'[6] (3 per cent. of the total population).

SIERRA LEONE. Registration is compulsory in the 'Colony' with 100,000 inhabitants, comprising about 6 per cent. of the total population. But many births outside Freetown escape registration 'owing to the absence of machinery for enforcing registration'.[7] Even in Freetown (60,000 inhabitants) the birth records do not seem to be complete, but 'the figures for deaths occurring in Freetown can be taken as fairly accurate'.[8] 'As registration is not compulsory

1 *Colonial Report*, 1785, *Gold Coast, 1935-6*, p. 8.

2 *Annual Summary and Report of the Principal Registrar of Births, Deaths and Burials of the Gold Coast, 1935*, pp. 1-2.

3 See 'Notes on Vital Statistics in Africa,' p. 126.

4 *Colonial Report*, 1763, *Nigeria, 1935*, p. 10.

5 Nigeria, *Annual Report on the Medical Services, 1935*, p. 7.

6 *Colonial Report*, 1769, *Northern Rhodesia, 1935*, p. 8.

7 *Colonial Report*, 1757, *Sierra Leone, 1935*, p. 12.

8 Ibid., p. 14.

there are no reliable figures available for births and deaths in the Protectorate '.[1]

SOUTH WEST AFRICA. 'The inhabitants of Native Reserves are required to report the births and deaths which occur therein.'[2] Births and deaths are registered also in the Eastern portion of the Caprivi Zipfel. 'There is no record of native births and deaths in other parts of the Territory.'[3] The entire registration area comprises about 30,000 people or 9 per cent. of the total population. The results indicate that registration is quite incomplete.

SUDAN. 'In principle, the registration of vital statistics covers the whole country, but does not furnish sufficiently reliable data except in the provinces of Khartoum, Berber, Dongola and in the Wadi Halfa district.'[4] But it is doubtful whether even in these provinces registration of births or deaths is adequate.

3. So far as we are aware, compulsory birth and death registration has not been introduced at all for natives in Angola,[5] Basutoland,[6] Bechuanaland,[7] Belgian Congo,[8] the British Cameroons,[9] Cape Verde Islands, Eritrea,

[1] *Colonial Report*, 1757, *Sierra Leone, 1935*, p. 12. See also P. Granville Edge, *Medical and Sanitary Reports from British Colonies, Protectorates and Dependencies for the Year 1934*, Tropical Diseases Bulletin, Supplement, October 1936, p. 25*. (This annual survey is a most valuable source of information about vital statistics in the British Colonial Empire.)

[2] *Report to the Council of the League of Nations concerning the Administration of South West Africa for the Year 1935*, p. 90.

[3] Ibid., p. 91.

[4] 'Notes on Vital Statistics in Africa', p. 182. See also Laffont, p. 28.

[5] According to *Boletim Trimestral da Repartição Central de Estatística Geral* 1934, p. 115, 4,231 births and 7,399 deaths were registered in 1933. These figures apparently include a few cases of native births and deaths.

[6] See Basutoland, *Annual Medical and Sanitary Report, 1935*, p. 5: 'Registration of births, deaths and marriages are only recorded for Europeans living in the country but not for any section of the native population.'

[7] See 'Notes on Vital Statistics in Africa', p. 174: 'The registration of births is not compulsory and, in practice, only exists for whites and half-castes.' See also *Colonial Report*, 1792, *Bechuanaland Protectorate, 1935*, p. 6: 'No vital statistics are available. The vast area of the Territory, with a widely scattered population and a relatively small number of officials, has made it impossible for the Government to collect data which would be of any value.'

[8] In 1934 and 1935 the registered native births numbered 769 and 2,103, and the registered native deaths 2,197 and 707; see *Rapport annuel sur l'administration de la Colonie du Congo Belge pendant l'année 1935*, p. 172.

[9] See *Report to the Council of the League of Nations on the Administration of the British Cameroons for the Year 1928*, p. 105: 'Registration of births and deaths has been continued in selected areas, but the results have proved no more satisfactory than those of previous years and figures are still so patently inaccurate as to be of no statistical value.' No later report mentioned even this optional registration of births and deaths, which was started in 1926 (see *Report, 1926*, p. 101).

French Equatorial Africa,[1] Kenya,[2] Libya,[3] French Morocco,[4] Mozambique,[5] Northern Africa, Nyasaland,[6] Portuguese Guinea, Rio de Oro, Ruanda-Urundi, St. Thomé and Principe, (French) Somali Coast, British Somaliland, Italian Somaliland, Spanish Guinea, Swaziland,[7] Tanganyika,[8] Tangier, and French Togoland.

America

Compulsory birth and death registration has been introduced in nearly all colonies, the only exceptions apparently being Alaska and the Panama Canal Zone. In some areas, such as Puerto Rico, registration probably is not quite complete.

Asia

1. Compulsory birth and death registration has been introduced for the whole area of the Aegean Islands, Brunei, Ceylon, Cyprus, the Federated Malay States, Formosa, French India, Hong Kong, Korea, Kwantung, North Borneo, Palestine, the Philippines, Saghalien, Straits Settlements, Trans-Jordan, and the Unfederated Malay States.

[1] See 'Notes on Vital Statistics in Africa', p. 138: 'Even at Brazzaville, the declaration of births is only general for Europeans. In 1928, for a native population of 10,993, only 24 births were recorded as against 224 deaths.'

[2] See *Colonial Report*, 1771, *Kenya Colony and Protectorate, 1935*, p. 11: 'It has not been possible to provide for the registration and notification of births and deaths among Africans.' Even for non-natives 'no reliable returns of births and deaths are available' (ibid., p. 9).

[3] Registration is not compulsory, but numerous births and deaths apparently are recorded. See Laffont, p. 25; 'Notes on Vital Statistics in Africa', p. 126.

[4] Registration is not compulsory for Moslems and defective for all but French; see Bunle, p. 651; 'Notes on Vital Statistics in Africa', p. 124; Jacques Le Meur, 'Le peuplement européen au Maroc', *Bulletin économique du Maroc*, July 1935, p. 180; 'Résultats provisoires du recensement du 8 mars 1936,' Ibid., July 1936, p. 256.

[5] Birth and death registration became compulsory for all but natives by order of 21 August 1930; see *Anuário de Lourenço Marques, 1934*, p. 120 E.

[6] See Nyasaland Protectorate, *Report on Native Affairs, 1933*, p. 29: 'The experiment in registration of births and deaths in the Fort Manning district begun by the medical department in 1932 was continued. It should be borne in mind that the native staff collecting statistics have no status, and no legal obligation falls upon the headmen to supply accurate information. It is to be expected, therefore, that a considerable margin of error may exist.'

[7] See Swaziland, *Annual Medical and Sanitary Report, 1935*, p. 4: 'General Native Population. Registration is not compulsory and no figures can be given about birth and death rates.' See also Ibid., p. 11: 'The only records are those of the births and deaths of Europeans.'

[8] See Tanganyika Territory, *Blue Book, 1933*, p. 120: 'Registration is compulsory for Europeans only and optional in the case of others.'

BRUNEI. Until quite recently the vital statistics were considered to be complete. The *Colonial Report* for 1933 still stated: 'Birth and death registration is compulsory and the figures are reliable.'[1] But when in the following year the death rate rose from 26·38 to 37·51, this increase was attributed exclusively to improved registration. 'Investigation has suggested that there has been no real increase in mortality, but that registration is yearly becoming more complete.'[2] The infant mortality rate had risen at the same time from 216 to 355; 'the explanation lies undoubtedly in the fact that the information upon which previous statistics were based, although considered to be complete, was in fact far from being so'. In 1935, however, the death rate dropped to 23·78 (and the infant mortality rate to 210). 'General health was undoubtedly better than in the previous year, and it is considered that registration of deaths in populous areas is practically complete: that registration is incomplete in the more distant areas is known, but the extent of error is unknown.'[3]

CEYLON. 'The birth and death statistics are very nearly exact.'[4]

FEDERATED MALAY STATES. Registration is still incomplete.[5]

FRENCH INDIA. According to Bunle (1925), the figures 'are certainly incomplete, particularly for the births'.[6]

HONG KONG. Until 1932 births and deaths were 'registered in the Colony proper and in New Kowloon but not in the New Territories outside New Kowloon'.[7] 'Since 1932 registration of Births and Deaths in the New Territories has been more and more fully enforced. The introduction of the new Births and Deaths Ordinance in the latter half of 1934 by improving facilities for registration on the one hand and checking on the other brought about an appreciable increase in registrations. This was particularly noticeable in the New Territories where the births registered were 3,810 as compared to 587 in 1932.'[8] Birth registration, on the whole,

[1] *Colonial Report*, 1662, *State of Brunei*, *1933*, p. 8. Literally the same, Ibid., 1624, *State of Brunei*, *1932*, p. 4.

[2] Ibid., 1751, *State of Brunei*, *1934*, p. 7. The *Annual Report on the Medical Department*, *1934*, p. 6, pointed out 'that the increase in the number of deaths registered has taken place only in those districts where registration is easy and a registry near at hand'.

[3] Ibid., 1753, *State of Brunei*, *1935*, p. 7.

[4] *Vital Statistics, Report of the Registrar-General of Ceylon for 1935*, p. 5.

[5] See *Colonial Report*, 1735, *Federated Malay States*, *1934*, p. 9.

[6] Bunle, p. 697.

[7] *Colonial Report*, 1585, *Hong Kong*, *1931*, p. 5.

[8] Ibid., 1775, *Hong Kong*, *1935*, p. 5.

apparently still in 1935 was rather deficient even for the non-Chinese population, but death registration seems to be fairly complete for all sections of the population.

PALESTINE. 'The registration of births and deaths is compulsory under the Public Health Ordinance of 1918, and though there certainly has occurred and probably still occurs omission to register, the degree of precision which has now been obtained in the settled population is very satisfactory and comparable with that obtaining in many European States. For obvious reasons registration is not effective in the nomadic Beduin tribes and for this reason this group is excluded from the figures on which the published statistics are based.'[1]

TRANS-JORDAN. 'Even at present, especially amongst the Beduin tribes, a number of births and deaths are not notified.'[2]

UNFEDERATED MALAY STATES. Registration is still imperfect, for example in the State of Kelantan.[3]

2. Compulsory birth and death registration has been introduced for natives in some parts of French Indo-China, Kwang Chau Wan, and Netherlands Indies.

FRENCH INDO-CHINA. Compulsory registration of native births and deaths was introduced in Cochinchina in 1884, in the urban centres of Annam in 1913, in Tonkin in 1924,[4] and in some sections of Cambodia in 1928.[5] But outside of Cochinchina registration is said to be very deficient, and even in Cochinchina it is incomplete, particularly in the rural districts.[6] Births of girls evidently very often are not registered.[7]

KWANG CHAU WAN. According to Bunle (1925), 'the statistics of births and deaths among the non-white population are still defective and apply only to an unknown fraction of the population (probably one-third).'[8]

1 *Report to the Council of the League of Nations on the Administration of Palestine and Trans-Jordan for the Year 1933*, pp. 135-6.

2 Ibid., *1935*, p. 322.

3 See *Colonial Report*, 1672, *State of Kelantan, 1933*, p. 7; Ibid., 1754, *State of Kelantan, 1935*, p. 7.

4 See Bunle, pp. 678, 682, 687, 689, 691, 693.

5 See Cazanove, p. 66.

6 See Bunle, pp. 678-9, 682-4, 689, 691-2; Brenier, pp. 9, 36; Cazanove, pp. 66, 68, 73; Henri Ulmer, 'Quelques données statistiques sur l'Indochine française,' *Bulletin de la Statistique générale de la France*, January-March, 1934, pp. 275-6.

7 See *Annuaire statistique de l'Indochine* 1931-2, p. 58, 1932-3, p. 50; *Bulletin économique de l'Indochine*, January-April, 1933, pp. 223-5.

8 Bunle, p. 694.

NETHERLANDS INDIES. Birth and death registration is compulsory in Java and Madura, comprising about two-thirds of the total population. In the Outer Provinces the registration area covers only about one-tenth of the population,[1] and registration there is very incomplete.

3. So far as we are aware, compulsory birth and death registration has not been introduced at all for natives in Aden and Perim, the Kuria Muria Islands, Macao, the Maldive Islands, Portuguese India, Sarawak, Socotra, Syria and Lebanon, and Timor.

EUROPE

Birth and death registration is compulsory in all colonies (Gibraltar, Malta, Spitzbergen).

OCEANIA

1. Compulsory birth and death registration has been introduced for the whole area of the Caroline, Marianne and Marshall Islands, the Cook Islands and Niue, the Fiji Islands, the Gilbert and Ellice Islands, Guam, Hawaii, Nauru, New Caledonia, Norfolk, the Tokelau Islands, Tonga, and Western Samoa.

2. Compulsory birth and death registration has been introduced for natives in six districts of the British Solomon Islands, comprising about three-sevenths of the total population,[2] and on a number of islands belonging to the French Settlements.[3]

3. So far as we are aware, compulsory birth and death registration has not been introduced at all for natives in American Samoa, New Guinea, the New Hebrides, and Papua.

[1] See *Netherlands Indian Report 1935, II Statistical Abstract for the Year 1934*, pp. 60-1.

[2] See *Colonial Report*, 1790, *British Solomon Islands Protectorate, 1935*, p. 4. See also British Solomon Islands Protectorate, *Annual Medical and Sanitary Report for 1935*, p. 2: 'Unfortunately births and deaths are not recorded in all Districts.'

[3] See Bunle, pp. 700-1; Brenier, p. 40; Cazanove, pp. 60-3.

Appendix

NOTES TO TABLES III, IV AND VII

Africa

Algeria.

(1) 8 March 1931 ; Statistique générale de la France, *Résultats statistiques du recensement général de la population, 1931*, vol. I, part I, p. 114.

(2) to (5) *Year-Book League of Nations, 1932-3* to *1935-6*. Population, June 1934 : 6,910,544 (Gouvernement général de l'Algérie, *Recensement démographique quinquennal du 8 mars 1931, Statistique de la population algérienne*, vol. I, p. 3.

(6) Census 8 March 1936 ; *Journal Officiel de l'Algérie*, 30 October 1936, quoted from *Questions Nord-Africaines*, No. 7, 25 December 1936, p. 71.

(7) *Résultats du recensement, 1931*, vol. I, part I, pp. 113-14; Gouvernement général de l'Algérie, *Recensements quinquennaux de la population algérienne de 1926 et de 1931*, pp. 18-19, 69, 129 ; Julien Franc, ' La population de l'Algérie en 1931,' *Bulletin de la Société de Géographie d'Alger et de l'Afrique du Nord*, vol. XXXVII, 1932, pp. 155-7. (I) Municipal population : (1) Europeans : 733,242 French (133,128 French from France, 425,602 French of colonial origin, 98,646 native Jews, 75,866 naturalized French including 5,836 Native Moslems) ; 148,342 Foreigners (109,821 Spaniards, 26,136 Italians, 3,706 Anglo-Maltese, 8,679 Others) ; (2) Natives : 5,548,236 French subjects, including 2,664 native Jews ; 40,078 Foreigners (33,840 Moroccans, 2,918 Tunisians, 3,320 Others). (II) Population counted separately (army, hospitals, school boarders) : 39,204 Europeans ; 44,349 Natives.

(8) *Statistique de la population algérienne*, vol. I, p. 3 : 953,436 Europeans ; 5,957,108 Natives.

(9) *Journal officiel de l'Algérie*, 30 October 1936 : 987,252 Europeans ; 6,247,432 Natives.

The ' French of colonial origin ' include a certain number of non-whites (descendants of naturalized natives ; possibly also descendants of other naturalized non-whites, children born in Algeria of foreign non-whites, and French non-white citizens of other colonies. The naturalized French also include a certain number of non-whites (naturalized natives; possibly also other naturalized non-whites). The foreign 'Europeans' comprise all non-native foreigners. We have counted 87 per cent. of the 'Europeans' as Whites and 13 per cent. as Natives (including Jews).

Angola.

(1) 31 December 1929; *Year-Book League of Nations, 1935-6.*

(2) to (5) *Year-Book League of Nations, 1932-3* to *1935-6.*

The figures are most uncertain, as will be seen from the following additional estimates:

1924	3,445,902	(Colônia de Angola, *Boletim Trimestral da Repartição Central de Estatística Geral 1934*, p. 114).
1925	4,120,000	(*Year-Book League of Nations, 1926*).
1926	4,150,000	(*Year-Book League of Nations, 1927*).
1927	2,887,054	(*Boletim, 1934*, p. 114).
31 Dec. 1927	5,100,000	(*Year-Book League of Nations, 1928*).
31 Dec. 1928	2,512,000	(*Year-Book League of Nations, 1929*).
1929	4,181,730	(Colónia de Moçambique, *Anuário Estatístico, 1929*, p. 3).
31 Dec. 1929	2,586,086	(Moçambique, *Anuário Estatístico, 1932*, p. 3).
1931	2,599,166	(*Statesman's Year-Book, 1934*, p. 1,232).
1931	3,011,118	(*Boletim, 1934*, p. 114).
1931	4,199,850	(*Almanach de Gotha, 1936*, p. 1,282).
30 June 1933	3,098,281	(*Anuário do Império Colonial Português, 1935*, p. 64).
1934	3,225,015	(*Anuário Estatístico de Angola, 1934*).

(7) *Anuário do Império Colonial Português, 1935*, p. 64, gives for 30 June 1933: 58,698 Whites, 18,957 Mixed, and 3,020,626 Blacks. Department of Overseas Trade, *Economic Conditions in Angola*, March 1934, p. 33, states: 'The Portuguese population is estimated at between 40,000 and 50,000, including half-castes of European habits. The foreign white population in 1932 is given officially as follows: Germany 488, United Kingdom 258, South Africa 141, United States 121, Italy 95, Belgium 79, and total 1,461.' We have entered in Table V, 30,000 as Whites.

Basutoland.

(1) 3 May 1921; *Basutoland Census, 1921*, pp. 5-6. Natives: 'population enumerated,' 495,937; 'absentees at labour centres' (outside the Territory), 47,141; 'total population,' 543,078.

The population has frequently been overestimated in recent years. *Statistical Abstract for the British Empire 1926 to 1935* (p. 3) estimated it both for 1931 and for 31 December 1935 at 650,000. The Basutoland *Annual Medical and Sanitary Report, 1934* contained a graph indicating that the population in 1931 to 1934 was 698,000, 720,000, 740,000 and 728,000.

(2) to (4) *Year-Book League of Nations, 1932-3* to *1934-5*.

(5) *Colonial Reports Annual*, 1723, p. 5.

(6) 5 May 1936; Union of South Africa, *Census 1936, Preliminary Report (Figures revised to the 15th October, 1936)*, p. I. 'It is estimated that 70,000 Basuto were absent from the Territory' (*Dominions Office and Colonial Office List, 1937*, p. 206).

(7) *Basutoland Census, 1921*, pp. 5, 13: 1,603 Europeans; 172 Asiatics; 1,069 Coloured; 495,937 Natives (for details of classification, see Chapter II).

(8) *Census 1936, Preliminary Report*, p. i: 1,434 Europeans; 341 Asiatics; 1,259 Coloured; 559,377 Natives.

(9) *Basutoland Census, 1921*, p. 21.

Bechuanaland.

(1) 3 May 1921; Union of South Africa, *Census, 1921, Report*, p. 2.

(2) to (5) *Year-Book League of Nations, 1932-3* to *1935-6*.

(6) 5 May 1936; Union of South Africa, *Census 1936, Preliminary Report*, p. i.

The population prior to 1936 seems to have been grossly underestimated.

(7) *Census, 1921, Report*, p. 2: 1,743 Europeans; 52 Asiatics; 1,003 Coloured; 150,185 Natives (for details of classification, see Chapter II).

The European population for 1931 to 1935 has been estimated at 1,800, 1,626, 1,642, 1,660, and 1,690 respectively (*Colonial Report*, 1579, pp. 5-6; 1650, p. 6; 1687, p. 6; 1742, p. 6; 1792, p. 6).

(8) *Census 1936, Preliminary Report*, p. i: 1,899 Europeans; 66 Asiatics; 3,727 Coloured; 260,064 Natives.

Belgian Congo.

(2) to (4) *Rapport annuel sur l'administration de la Colonie du Congo Belge, 1931*, pp. 9, 99; *1932*, pp. 10, 101; *1933*, pp. 10, 128:

	31 Dec. 1931	*31 Dec. 1932*	*31 Dec. 1933*
Native population enumerated ..	8,880,881	8,956,462	8,972,283
Not enumerated, estimated ..	537,848	426,661	400,275
Total	9,418,729	9,383,123	9,372,558
Non-native population	22,482	18,721	17,588

(5) *Rapport, 1934*, pp. 12, 130: Enumerated Native population, 9,282,991 (no mention being made of not enumerated natives); Non-native population, 17,845.

(6) *Rapport, 1935*, pp. 17, 173: Enumerated Native population, 9,775,191 ('Taking account of the not enumcrated individuals who are mainly women and children, the total population of the Colony must be approximately 11,000,000 inhabitants'); White population 18,683.

(7) (8) *Rapport, 1931*, pp. 100-1; *1932*, pp. 102-3; *1933*, pp. 126-7; *1934*, pp. 128-9; *1935*, pp. 174-5. Non-Native population:

Nationality	*1 Jan. 1932*	*1 Jan. 1933*	*1 Jan. 1934*	*1 Jan. 1935*	*1 Jan. 1936*
Belgians	15,034	12,045	11,423	11,815	12,654
Other Europeans ..	6,307	5,609	5,112	5,059	5,061
United States ..	575	597	581	580	523
Canada	16	19	32	19	23
South Africa	325	242	216	195	166
Turkey	27	23	26	23	21
Others	198[1]	186[2]	198	154	235
Total	22,482	18,721	17,588	17,845	18,683

[1] 7 Uruguayans, 7 Brazilians, 13 Australians, 21 Egyptians, 112 Cypriots, 5 New Zealanders, 1 Bolivian, 5 Stateless, 27 Others.

[2] 8 Uruguayans, 9 Brazilians, 10 Australians, 23 Egyptians, 74 Cypriots, 30 Rhodians, 32 Others.

We have counted the Egyptians as Africans, the Turks, Cypriots and Rhodians as Asiatics and all others (with the exception of the Stateless and the Others) as Whites.

Cameroons (under British Mandate).

(1) 23 April 1931; *Census of Nigeria, 1931*, vol. I, p. 8.

(2) to (6) *Report to the Council of the League of Nations on the Administration of the Cameroons under British Mandate for the Year 1932*, pp. 99-100; *1933*, pp. 83-84; *1934*, pp. 110-11; *1935*, p. 115. *Statistical Abstract British Empire, 1926 to 1935*, p. 303, gives erroneously the 1935 figure for natives (817,616) as covering the whole population.

(7) to (11) *Report, 1932*, pp. 99-100; *1933*, pp. 83-4; *1934*, pp. 110-11; 1935, p. 115. Population subdivided into Europeans and Natives (comprising apparently all natives of Africa and also half-castes).

Cameroons (under French Mandate).

(1) 1 July 1931; *Rapport annuel au Conseil de la Société des Nations sur l'administration sous mandat du territoire du Cameroun pour l'année 1933*, p. 93 (according to ibid., *1931*, pp. 66-7, 2,225,961; *1932*, p. 125, 2,225,966).

(2) (3) *Year-Book League of Nations, 1932-3, 1933-4.*

(4) (5) (6) *Rapport, 1933*, p. 93; *1934*, p. 119; *1935*, p. 105.

(7) *Rapport, 1932*, p. 125; *1933*, p. 93: 2,164 'Europeans' (1,684 French, 374 other European nationalities, 76 Americans, 27 Libano-Syrians, 2 Armenians, 1 Turk); 2,199,802 Natives.

(8) *Rapport, 1933*, pp. 93, 95: 2,038 'Europeans' (1,578 French, 321 other European nationalities, 96 Americans, 4 Canadians, 34 Libano-Syrians, 4 Armenians, 1 Turk); 2,296,457 Natives.

(9) *Rapport, 1934*, pp. 119, 121: 2,106 'Europeans' (1,619 French, 344 other European nationalities, 83 Americans, 1 Canadian, 54 Libano-Syrians, 5 Armenians); 280 Half-castes; 2,227,815 Natives.

(10) *Rapport, 1935*, pp. 105, 110: 2,324 'Europeans' (1,761 French, 430 other European nationalities, 60 Americans, 4 Canadians, 63 Libano-Syrians, 4 Turks, 2 not stated); 286 Half-castes; 2,338,495 Natives.

Cape Verde Islands.

(1) (2) 31 December 1931; Colónia de Moçambique, *Anuário Estatistico, 1933*, p. 3.

(3) (4) *Anuário do Império Colonial Português, 1935*, pp. 3, 34.

(5) *Almanach de Gotha, 1937*, p. 1217.

(7) *Anuário do Império Colonial Português, 1935*, p. 34: 5,825 Whites; 60,134 Half-castes; 87,223 Blacks. Distribution by nationality: 656 Portuguese from the motherland; 152,040 Portuguese from Cape Verde Islands; 278 Portuguese from other Portuguese colonies; 208 Foreigners. We have counted the Portuguese from the motherland and the Foreigners as Europeans and all others as Africans.

Eritrea.

(1) 21 April 1931; *Annuario Statistico Italiano, 1936*, p. 260.

(2) to (5) *Year-Book League of Nations, 1932-3* to *1935-6*.

According to Istituto Centrale di Statistica del Regno d'Italia, *Censimento Generale della Popolazione 21 Aprile 1931*, vol. V, pp. 34, 41, the population was composed as follows: 4,188 Italians (including 515 Half-castes, see ibid., pp. *4, *14); 372 Foreigners (Nationality: 297 Greece, 48 other European, 22 Turkey, 1 French colonies in Asia, 2 Egypt, 2 United States); 596,013 Natives.

According to ibid., pp. 38, 42, the distribution by birthplace was as follows:

	Non-natives	*Foreign Residents*	
		Greeks	*Others*
Italy	2,355	—	3
Eritrea	1,865	157	31
Other Italian colonies	28	14	—
Abroad	309	120	33
Unknown	3	—	—
Total	4,560	291	67

French Equatorial Africa.

(1) 8 March 1931; Official evaluation.

(2) (3) *Year-Book League of Nations, 1932-3, 1933-4*.

(4) *Statesman's Year-Book, 1936*, p. 927.

(5) Agence Économique du Gouvernement général de l'Afrique Équatoriale Française, *Afrique Équatoriale Française* (1935), p. 4: 'about 3,430,000 Natives'.

(6) League of Nations, *Annual Epidemiological Report, 1935*, p. 65.

(7) Official evaluation: 4,687 'Europeans and Assimilated' (3,806 French, 256 Portuguese, 472 of another specified European

nationality, 57 Americans, 22 Syrians, and 74 others); 3,192,282 Natives. We have counted as Whites the French, one-half of the Portuguese, the other Europeans, and the Americans.

French West Africa.

(1) 1 July 1931; *Résultats statistiques du recensement général, 1931*, vol. I, part I, p. 115.

(2) *Year-Book League of Nations, 1932-3.*

(3) *Bulletin de l'agence générale des colonies, 1934*, pp. 322-3.

(4) Official evaluation.

(5) *Statesman's Year-Book, 1936*, p. 936.

(6) 8 March 1936; *Almanach de Gotha, 1937*, p. 1038.

(7) to (10) *Recensement, 1931*, vol. I, part I, p. 115; *Bulletin, 1934*, pp. 322-3; *Annuaire statistique de l'Afrique Occidentale Française, 1933-4*, p. 19:

	1 July 1931	*31 Dec. 1932*	*31 Dec. 1933*	*31 Dec. 1934*
French Whites ..	14,408	19,657	19,511	17,631
Foreign Europeans and Assimilated	6,680	7,629	7,820	7,088
French Native citizens	68,812	71,121	72,024	14,423,878 (French Native citizens and subjects together)
French Native subjects	14,454,917	14,365,150	14,282,245	
Foreign Native subjects	31,156	23,030	22,542	20,231
Total	14,575,973	14,486,587	14,404,142	14,468,828

(11) *Almanach de Gotha, 1937*, p. 1038: 24,798 Europeans (including 17,148 French).

We have counted one-quarter of the 'Foreign Europeans and Assimilated' as Whites and three-quarters as Asiatics (Syrians, etc.).

Gambia (Colony and Protectorate).

(1) 24 April 1931; *Report and Summary of the Census of the Gambia, 1931*, p. 6.

(2) (3) (5) *Year-Book League of Nations, 1932-3, 1933-4, 1935-6.*

(4) (6) *Statistical Abstract British Empire, 1924 to 1933*, p. 3, *1926 to 1935*, p. 3.

(7) *Census, 1931*, pp. 6-7. Colony: 274 Non-Africans, 14,096 Africans; Protectorate: population, 185,150. We have assumed

that the population of the Protectorate were all Africans. Of the 274 Non-Africans, 226 were reported with a European nationality, 2 as Americans, 2 as West Indians, 32 as Syrians, and 12 as 'Others'. Of the total population of the Colony, 25 British subjects and 32 Foreign subjects were born in Syria. We have assumed that the 2 Non-African West Indians were of European descent, that the 57 persons born in Syria were all Asiatics, and that the 12 'Others' were all of European descent (since Syria is the only Asiatic country listed as birthplace). We have therefore entered 217 as Europeans and 57 as Asiatics.

(8) *Census, 1931*, p. 8.

Gold Coast.

(1) 26 April 1931; *The Gold Coast, 1931, Appendices containing Comparative Returns and General Statistics of the 1931 Census*, p. 1.

(2) (3) (5) *Year-Book League of Nations, 1932-3, 1933-4, 1935-6.*

(4) (6) *Statistical Abstract British Empire, 1924 to 1933*, p. 3; *1926 to 1935*, p. 3.

According to *Annual Summary and Report of the Principal Registrar of Births, Deaths and Burials, 1932*, p. 9, *1933*, p. 13, *1934*, p. 13, *1935*, p. 11, Population 30 June 1932 to 1935: 2,964,627, 3,040,446, 3,116,264, 3,192,083.

(7) *The Gold Coast, 1931, Appendices*, pp. 1, 21, 23: 3,139 Non-Africans, 2,866,715 Africans. Of the Non-Africans, 2,440 (including 72 on ship-board) had a European nationality, 49 (including 32) were Americans, 20 West Indians, 1 Arabian, 1 Chinese, 56 Indians, 570 Syrians, and 2 Turks. The 20 West Indians were apparently of European descent since of the African immigrants only one is listed as having come from the West Indies. We have, therefore, allocated 2,509 to Europeans and 630 to Asiatics.

According to *Report on the Medical Department for the Year 1932-3*, p. 10, *1933-4*, p. 12, *1934*, p. 7, *1935*, p. 8, the resident 'European,' i.e. Non-African, population numbered:

30 June 1931 ..	3,508	30 June 1934	3,145
30 June 1932 ..	3,047	31 Dec. 1934	3,491
30 June 1933 ..	2,959	31 Dec. 1935	3,969

These figures which include the persons on leave are not comparable with the census results since the latter refer to the *de facto* population.

According to *Report of the Principal Registrar, 1932*, p. 9, *1933*, p. 13, *1934*, p. 13, *1935*, p. 11, the African population numbered:

30 June 1932 ..	2,961,488	30 June 1934	3,113,125
30 June 1933 ..	3,037,307	30 June 1935	3,188,944

Kenya.

(2) to (6) *Colonial Report*, 1606, p. 13; 1659, p. 13; 1688, p. 12; 1722, p. 12; 1771, p. 9. The figure for 1931 is an estimate for the date of the non-native census (6 March).

(7) *Report on the Non-Native Census Enumeration made in the Colony and Protectorate of Kenya on the Night of the 6th March, 1931*, pp. 9-10; *Colonial Report*, 1606, p. 13: 16,812 Europeans; 39,644 Indians; 3,979 Goans; 12,166 Arabs; 947 Coloured ('all those who were definitely returned as such' including 'Coloured Seychellois, Mauritians and Ceylonese'); 205 Half-castes ('crossing between non-native and native'); 194 Others ('Chinese, Japanese and any other non-European races'); 2,966,993 Natives. We have counted as Asiatics all Non-Natives except Europeans and Half-castes.

(8) to (11) *Colonial Report*, 1659, pp. 12-13; 1688, p. 12; 1722, p. 12; 1771, p. 9; *South and East African Year Book*, *1937*, p. 762:

	31 Dec. 1931	*31 Dec. 1932*	*31 Dec. 1933*	*31 Dec. 1934*	*31 Dec. 1935*	*30 June 1936*
Europeans ..	16,957	17,249	17,332	17,501	17,997	17,759
Indians ..	37,196	34,966	33,735	34,955	36,461	37,676
Goans ..	3,431	3,369	3,246	3,316	3,437	3,522
Arabs	11,751	11,752	11,932	12,131	12,599	12,841
Others ..	1,374	1,362	1,390	1,401	1,436	...
Natives ..	...	3,007,645	3,017,117	3,024,975	3,012,421	...

We have counted as Asiatics all Non-Natives except Europeans and except 15 per cent. of the 'Others'.

(12) *Non-Native Census, 1931*, pp. 108-12.

Libya.

(1) 21 April 1931; *Annuario Statistico Italiano, 1936*, p. 254.

(2) to (5) *Year-Book League of Nations, 1932-3* to *1935-6*.

(6) Census 21 April 1936; Istituto Centrale di Statistica del Regno d'Italia, *Notiziario demografico, 1937*, pp. 87-8. The increase was due in part to the concentration of Italian and Eritrean troops in Libya during the war against Ethiopia.

According to *Censimento Generale della Popolazione 21 Aprile 1931*, vol. V, pp. 12, 20, 24, 31, the population was composed as follows: 44,600 Italians; 4,807 Foreigners (Nationality: 2,048 British, 1,273 Greece, 1,046 French, 309 other European nationality, 89 Turkey, 10 British India, 4 French colonies in Asia, 11 Egypt, 10 French colonies in Africa, 4 United States, 1 Bolivia, 1 Uruguay, 1 New Zealand).

According to *Notiziario demografico, 1937*, pp. 87-8, there were on 21 April 1936 in Libya: 112,834 Italians; 2,803 Foreigners; 772,999 Natives.

According to *Censimento, 1931*, vol. V, pp. 17, 21, 28, 32, the distribution by birthplace was as follows:

	Non-natives	*Foreign Residents*			
		British	*French*	*Greek*	*Others*
Italy	33,782	15	3	13	10
Italian colonies ..	11,352	1,787	872	393	162
Abroad	4,170	226	146	241	151
Unknown ..	103	—	—	—	—
Total ..	49,407	2,028	1,021	647	323

Madagascar and Dependencies.

(1) 1 July 1931; *Bulletin de l'agence générale des colonies, 1933*, p. 338. Figure includes 9,032 Army and Navy (1,845 Europeans, 7,187 Natives).

(2) (5) *Year-Book League of Nations, 1932-3, 1935-6.*

(3) *Bulletin, 1934*, p. 568. Figure includes 5,306 Army and Navy (1,540 Europeans, 3,766 Natives).

(4) Official evaluation. Figure includes 6,778 Army and Navy (1,831 Europeans, 4,947 Natives).

(7) to (9) *Bulletin, 1933*, p. 338, *1934*, pp. 549, 568; Official evaluation:

	1 July 1931	*31 Dec. 1932*	*31 Dec. 1933*
Europeans:			
French born in France ..	9,256	10,124	10,528
French born in colonies ..	11,764	12,799	13,461
Foreigners	2,534	2,569[1]	2,465
Native French subjects ..	3,722,961	3,733,051	3,781,638
Native Foreign subjects			
British	753	377	192
Africans	566	956	941
Hindus	7,945	7,387	7,621
Chinese	2,517	2,246	2,487
Half-caste French	1,675	2,273	1,198
Half-caste Foreigners	530	787	456
Total	3,760,501	3,772,569	3,820,987

[1] 1,604 British, 307 Greek, 547 other European nationality, 91 Americans, 1 Argentine, 6 Canadians, 4 Armenians, 3 Libanese, 4 Syrians, 2 Turks.

We have counted as Whites the French born in France, the Foreign Europeans (except 13 counted as Asiatics), and two-thirds of the French born in colonies; as Asiatics the Hindus, the Chinese, and 13 of the Foreign 'Europeans'.

Mauritius and Dependencies.

(1) 26 April 1931; *Final Report on the Census Enumeration made in the Colony of Mauritius and its Dependencies on April 26th, 1931*, pp. 2, 3. Total is 'irrespective of the Military'. The 'Military in barracks' at the 1921 census numbered 206 (see *Final Report on the Census Enumeration, 1921*, p. 12).

(2) The population of the Colony was 391,044 (see *Colonial Report*, 1597, p. 7). The population of the Dependencies was 9,659 on 26 April 1931 and was estimated at 9,937 on 31 December 1932 (Colony of Mauritius, *Annual Report of the Registrar-General on Births, Deaths and Marriages for 1932*, p. 3).

(3) *Report of the Registrar-General, 1932*, p. 3.

(4) to (6) *Colonial Report*, 1685, p. 7; 1731, p. 7; 1770, p. 8.

(7) *Census, 1931*, p. 6. Population of Mauritius: 645 Europeans; 115,021 Mauritians; 268,649 Indians; 8,923 Chinese. For details of classification, see Chapter II. It should be noted, however, that the 'Indians', contrary to the definition of the term, included 14,953 Christians (see ibid., p. 19).

The population of the Dependencies was given as 9,303 'General population,' 221 Indians, and 135 Chinese (ibid., p. 3).

The figure of 645 Europeans entered in the Table comprises only civilians in Mauritius.

We have entered 300,000 as Asiatics.

The following data are compiled from *Colonial Report*, 1597, p. 7; *Report of the Registrar-General, 1932*, p. 3; *1933*, p. 3; *1934*, pp. 3, 11-12; *1935*, pp. 3, 11-12.

	31 Dec. 1931	*31 Dec. 1932*	*31 Dec. 1933*	*31 Dec. 1934*		*31 Dec. 1935*	
	Maur.	*Maur.*	*Maur.*	*Maur.*	*Dep.*	*Maur.*	*Dep.*
General Pop. ..	116,502	117,223	118,698	119,955	} 10,130	121,237	} 10,433
Chinese ..	8,746	8,749	8,428	8,349		8,485	
Indians ..	265,796	262,428	263,571	265,429	327	266,545	320

The General Population is said to cover 'Europeans and descendants of Europeans and people of African and mixed origin', the Chinese 'Chinese immigrants and their descendants', and the Indians 'Indian immigrants and their descendants', but the General Population very likely includes a number of pure-blooded descendants of Indian immigrants.

(8) *Census, 1931*, pp. 13-14. Figures refer to Mauritius.

Morocco (French).

(1) 8 March 1931; *Résultats statistiques du recensement général, 1931*, vol. I, part I, p. 114; *Résultats statistiques globaux du recensement de la population de la zone française du Maroc, 1931*, pp. 2-3. The census was incomplete (see Jacques Le Meur, 'Le peuplement européen au Maroc,' *Bulletin économique du Maroc*, July 1935, p. 179).

(2) to (5) *Year-Book League of Nations, 1932-3* to *1935-6*.

(6) 8 March 1936 (Census); *Bulletin économique du Maroc*, July 1936, Table following, p. 256. 'The Moslem Moroccans were enumerated under the auspices of the local authorities. It results from the verifications that the percentage of ascertained errors or omissions does, in general, not exceed 2 per cent.' (ibid., p. 255).

(7) *Résultats statistiques du recensement géneral, 1931*, vol. I, part I, p. 114; *Resensement de la population de la zone française du Maroc, 1931*, pp. 2-3, 6. I. Civilians: 128,177 French (115,628 French citizens, 11,683 French subjects, 866 French Protected non-Moroccans); 44,304 Foreigners (22,684 Spaniards, 12,602 Italians, 8,583 other European nationalities including Americans, 54 Egyptians, 124 Turks, 44 Palestinians, 49 Armenians, 15 Persians, 148 not stated); 4,709,229 Moroccans (4,591,624 Moslems, 117,605 Jews). II. Population of the unsubdued zone: 483,099 (476,119 Moslems, 6,980 Jews). III. Military: 40,051 (non-Moroccans). We have counted as Whites the French civilian citizens, one-half of the Foreign civilians, and the whole Military.

(8) *Bulletin économique du Maroc*, July 1936, Table following, p. 256. I. Civilians: 155,569 French (139,131 French citizens, 15,757 French subjects, 681 French Protected non-Moroccans); 50,937 Foreigners (23,414 Spaniards, 15,645 Italians, 11,878 other nationalities); 6,036,200 Moroccans (5,874,888 Moslems, 161,312 Jews). II. Military: 21,480 French (15,111 French citizens, 5,730 French subjects, 639 French Protected non-Moroccans); 8,616 Foreigners; 23,334 Moroccans (Moslems). We have counted as Whites the French civilian citizens, one-half of the Foreign civilians, and the non-Moroccan Military.

The birthplaces of the non-Moroccan civilians on 8 March 1931, were as follows (*Recensement de la population de la zone française du Maroc, 1931*, p. 13) :

	French	*Foreigners*
France	57,674	470
French Morocco ..	27,291	10,367
Algeria	31,662	3,100
Tunis	2,502	3,106
Other French Colonies	1,196	126
Abroad	4,042	26,575
Not stated	3,810	560
Total	128,177	44,304

Morocco (Spanish).

(2) *Year-Book League of Nations, 1932-3.*

(3) (4) *Boletín de la Sociedad Geografica Nacional, 1934*, p. 342.

(5) *Statesman's Year-Book, 1936*, p. 1,138.

(8) According to *Boletín, 1934*, p. 342, in 1932 : 38,005 Spaniards, 666,536 Moslems, 12,050 Jews, 438 Foreigners ; in 1933 : 32,804 Spaniards, 673,876 Moslems, 12,988 Jews, 605 Foreigners. According to *Statesman's Year-Book, 1936*, p. 1,138, in 1934 : 'about 44,379 Europeans and 12,918 Jews.'

Mozambique.

(2) to (5) *Year-Book League of Nations, 1932-3* to *1935-6*.

(6) League of Nations, *Annual Epidemiological Report, 1935*, p. 65. Non-Native Census, 3 May 1928 (Colónia de Moçambique, *Anuário Estatístico, 1933*, pp. 42-4) : 17,842 Whites (17,765 of European nationality, 43 Americans, 19 Brazilians, 2 Egyptians, 11 Syrians, 2 Turks) ; 8,357 Half-castes (2 Afghan, 6 American, 637 British, 15 Chinese, 6 Dutch, 20 French, 2 German, 12 Greek, 13 Italian, 7,644 Portuguese) ; 896 Yellow (887 Chinese, 1 Japanese, 8 Portuguese) ; 3,478 Portuguese Indians ; 4,997 British Indians.

Non-Native Census, 2 May 1935 (Colónia de Moçambique, *Boletim Económico e Estatístico*, March 1936, p. 2 ; *Moçambique Documentário Trimestral*, September 1935, pp. 144-5) : 23,131 Europeans ; 13,259 Half-castes ; 1,056 Yellow ; 4,484 Natives of Portuguese India ; 3,820 Natives of British India.

Native census, 1 August 1930 (*Boletim Económico*, March 1936, p. 2): 3,960,261.

Native (Black) population, estimated 1932 (*Anuário do Império Colonial Português, 1935*, p. 3): 3,993,176.

Nigeria.

(1) 23 April 1931; *Census of Nigeria, 1931*, vol. I, p. 8. The total population including Cameroons under British Mandate was 19,928,171. The Government Statistician, taking account of omissions, estimated the population (including Mandated Territory) at 22,000,000. 'This estimate is more likely to err in defect than in excess' (ibid., p. 23). Nigeria, *Annual Report on the Medical Services, 1935*, p. 7, gives 19,928,171 erroneously as the figure for the 'non-European' population.

(2) (3) *Year-Book League of Nations, 1932-3, 1933-4.*

(4) *Statistical Abstract British Empire, 1924 to 1933*, p. 3.

(5) (6) According to Colony and Protectorate of Nigeria, *Blue Book for the Year ending 31st December, 1934*, Section 15, p. 2, ibid., *1935*, Section 15, p. 2, the 'Coloured Native Population' (including Mandated Territory) was 19,865,452 and 19,918,516 respectively. The Native Population of the Mandated Territory was 778,352 and 817,616. According to *Annual Report on the Medical Services, 1935*, p. 8, the European population (apparently including Mandated Territory) was 5,021 and 5,246. We have assumed that the non-European non-Natives were the same as at the census of 1931 (490). The figures for the 'Coloured Native Population' are frequently supposed to cover the whole population; see, for example, *Statistical Abstract British Empire, 1926 to 1935*, p. 3; *Statesman's Year-Book, 1936*, p. 268.

(7) *Census of Nigeria, 1931*, pp. 9-10, 32. Nigeria (including Mandated Territory): 4,952 White races ('Europeans, Americans and persons of European or American extraction, whatever their nationality'); 490 Asiatics; 19,895,522 Natives of Nigeria ('Persons descended from a tribe indigenous to Nigeria'); 27,207 Native Foreigners (Persons 'descended from other African Tribes'). The population of the Mandated Territory was 797,312; the European population numbered 281 on 31 December 1930 and 278 on 31 December 1931.

The European population on 31 December 1931 to 1935 was: 4,882, 4,375, 4,729, 5,021, and 5,246 (*Annual Report on the Medical Services, 1933*, p. 10; *1935*, p. 8).

Northern Africa.

(1) 31 December 1930; *Censo de la Población de España, 1930*, vol. I, p. 330.

(2) to (5) *Year-Book League of Nations, 1932-3* to *1935-6*.

(7) *Censo, 1930*, vol. I, pp. 370-87. Figures include 297 Whites enumerated in Rio de Oro.

Northern Rhodesia.

(1) 5 May 1931; Northern Rhodesia, *Report of the Director of Census regarding the Census taken on the 5th May, 1931*, pp. 35, 43. 'The census did not include the native population, but District Officers were asked to supply figures showing the population as estimated in their reports for the year 1930, less deductions based on calculations of the number of those who were absent from the Territory on Census night.' The deductions thus made amounted to 36,148.

(2) to (5) *Year-Book League of Nations, 1932-3* to *1935-6*.

Europeans, 31 December 1932 to 1935: 10,553, 11,278, 11,464, 9,913 (*Colonial Report*, 1769, p. 8; Northern Rhodesia, *Blue Book for the Year ended 31 December 1935*, Section O, p. 2).

Asiatics, 31 December 1933 to 1935: 179, 188, 227. All these Asiatics were British Indians with the exception of 3 Seychellois in 1933 and 1934. (*Colonial Report*, 1669, p. 9; 1721, p. 9; 1769, p. 9.)

Native population, 31 December 1931 to 1934: 1,372,235, 1,382,705, 1,371,213, 1,366,425. 'No count of the population was made in 1935 but the figures are believed to be about the same as in 1934.' (*Colonial Report*, 1769, p. 8.) These figures apparently include absentees but do not include 'Coloured'.

(7) *Census, 1931*, pp. 35, 43: 13,846 Europeans; 176 Asiatics (Goanese, Syrians, Japanese, Chinese, Arabs, and Afghans); 425 Coloured; 1,295,081 Natives. For further details of classification, see Chapter II.

(8) *Census, 1931*, pp. 77-80, 90, 93.

Nyasaland.

(1) 26 April 1931; Nyasaland Protectorate, *Report on the Census of 1931*, p. 13. *De jure* census for natives ('the native enumerators visited every village in the areas assigned to them and counted every native permanently domiciled therein, whether in fact that native was actually present, or whether he was away abroad or even in another part of the Protectorate'; ibid., p. 6).

(2) *Year-Book League of Nations, 1932-3.* In *Statistical Abstract British Empire, 1925 to 1931*, p. 3, the population on 31 December 1931 is estimated at only 1,502,283.

(3) to (6) *Colonial Report*, 1658, pp. 6-7; 1665, p. 6; 1739, p. 6; 1776, p. 6.

(7) *Census, 1931*, pp. 9, 12-13, Table H: 1,975 Europeans ('persons of European extraction'); 1,591 Asiatics (1,509 British Indians, 5 Singalese, 73 Portuguese Indians, 1 Arab, 3 Chinese); 1,599,888 Natives ('any native of Africa not of European or Asiatic extraction').

(8) to (11) *Colonial Report*, 1658, pp. 6-7; 1665, p. 6; 1739, p. 6; 1776, p. 6.

(12) *Census, 1931*, Tables B, I.

Portuguese Guinea.

(1) 1931; *Anuário do Império Colonial Português, 1935*, p. 3 (1928 census of civilized population and 1931 census of native population).

(2) (3) (5) *Year-Book League of Nations, 1932-3, 1933-4, 1935-6.*

(4) *Statesman's Year-Book, 1937*, p. 1253.

(6) League of Nations, *Annual Epidemiological Report, 1935*, p. 65.

(7) *Anuário, 1935*, p. 3: 983 Whites; 1,310 Half-castes; 362,610 Blacks; 26 Yellows.

Réunion.

(1) 1 July 1931; *Bulletin de l'agence économique des colonies, 1934*, p. 1227.

(2) to (5) *Year-Book League of Nations, 1932-3* to *1935-6.*

(6) Census 1 July 1936; League of Nations, *Annual Epidemiological Report, 1935*, p. 65.

(7) *Bulletin, 1934*, p. 1227; *Résultats statistiques du recensement général, 1931*, vol. I, part I, p. 113: 192,961 Europeans and Assimilated (192,566 French, 395 Foreigners); 4,972 Others (921 Madagascans, 302 Kaffirs, 1,311 Arabs, 196 British Indians, 2,242 Chinese). According to the enumeration of 31 December 1848, the last one to consider colour, the resident population consisted of 37,290 Whites and 66,201 Coloured (*Tableaux de population*, etc., 1848, p. 19).

Rio de Oro, including Ifni.

(2) to (5) *Year-Book League of Nations, 1932-3* to *1935-6.*

White population, Census, 31 December 1930: 297 (*Censo de la Población de España, 1930*, vol. I, p. 330).

Ruanda-Urundi.

(2) to (6) *Rapport au Conseil de la Société des Nations au sujet de l'administration du Ruanda-Urundi, 1935*, p. 251.

(7) to (11) *Rapport, 1932*, pp. 20-1 ; *1933*, pp. 26-7 ; *1935*, pp. 32-3, 251 :

	31 Dec. 1931	*31 Dec. 1932*	*31 Dec. 1933*	*31 Dec. 1934*	*31 Dec. 1935*
Europeans ..	904	811	803	868	893
Mulattoes ..	60	79	91	99	114
Abyssinians ..	1	1	1	1	1
Afghans ..	1	1	10	10	1
Arabs	307	179	214	221	247
Baluchis ..	12	11	12	11	10
Hindus	186	201	222	193	209
Madagascans ..	—	1	1	1	1
Senegalese ..	3	3	2	2	9
Others[1]	87	242	202	198	226
Natives ..	3,450,000	3,450,000	3,035,130	3,291,665	3,385,583

[1] Other 'Asiatics and Coloured, including children born of unions between Asiatics and native women, not recognized by their fathers'.

We have counted as Asiatics the Afghans, Arabs, Baluchis, Hindus, and one-half of the 'Others'.

St. Helena and Dependencies.

(1) 26 April 1931 ; *Colonial Report*, 1777, pp. 6-7. St. Helena, 3995 ; Ascension, 188. Figure for St. Helena includes the Garrison, according to *Census of the Island of St. Helena in 1931*, Table No. I.

(2) *Statistical Abstract British Empire, 1925 to 1931*, p. 3 ; *Colonial Report*, 1568, p. 5.

(3) *Year-Book League of Nations, 1933-4.*

(4) to (6) *Colonial Report*, 1677, pp. 5-6; 1736, p. 6; 1777, pp. 6-7. According to *Colonial Report*, 1777, pp. 6-7, there were on 26 April 1931, on both islands, 4,003 St. Helenians, 178 other British residents, 2 other nationals. According to *Census, 1931*, Table No. VI, 3,851 of the population of St. Helena were born in St. Helena, 106 in the United Kingdom, 3 in Ireland, 31 in British colonies, 1 in Portuguese East Africa, 1 in West Africa, 1 in United States of America, 1 in Brazil.

The figures for St. Helena and Dependencies do not include the Island Tristan da Cunha which, according to a census taken on 9 January 1932 by the Captain of H.M.S. *Carlisle*, had 163 inhabitants. 'In November 1933, the population numbered 167, all with the exception of 6 having been born in the Island' (*Dominions Office and Colonial Office List, 1937*, p. 523).

St. Thomé and Principe Islands.

(1) December 1921; *Anuário do Império Colonial Português, 1935*, p. 3.

(2) to (5) *Year-Book League of Nations, 1932-3* to *1935-6.*

According to *Anuário, 1935*, p. 3: 1,118 Whites; 795 Half-castes; 57,125 Blacks; 22 Yellows.

Seychelles.

(1) 26 April 1931; Colony of Seychelles, *Census for the Year 1931*, p. 1.

(2) to (6) *The Seychelles Blue Book for the Year 1931*, p. 95; *1932*, p. 102; *1933*, p. 102; *1934*, p. 107; *1935*, p. 105.

According to *Census, 1931*, pp. 4-6: 26,706 'Europeans, and persons of European descent and Africans'; 503 Indians; 235 Chinese. 'The whole population of the Colony can come under these headings; it was found impossible, and it would certainly have been invidious, to classify the population according to colour.'

(8) *Census for the Year 1931*, pp. 5-6, 43.

Sierra Leone.

(1) 26 April 1931; Sierra Leone, *Report of Census for the Year 1931*, pp. 19, 73. Figure includes 151 persons on board ships in harbour.

(2) to (5) *Year-Book League of Nations, 1932-3* to *1935-6.*

(6) *Economic Survey of the Colonial Empire* (*1935*), p. 139.

(7) *Census, 1931*, pp. 4, 8, 10, 19, 47, 59, 166: 651 Europeans (598 of European nationality, 53 Americans); 35,892 Sierra Leoneans (Colony non-Native Africans as distinguished from Protectorate native tribesmen and native 'foreigners'; classified in previous censuses as 'Liberated Africans and their descendants'); 102 West Indians; 290 'Mulattos' (including 143 Syrian-Africans and also some European-Asiatics); 756 other Africans, Non-Natives (Liberians, American Negroes, and Africans from other Colonies); 1,729,573 African Native Tribes; 25 Indians; 1,166 Syrians; 23 Arabs ('so-called Arabs who are really Moors'); 2 Asiatic Greeks. These figures do not include the 151 persons on board ships (67 Europeans, 84 Africans).

(8) *Census, 1931*, pp. 49, 60, 66, 168-9, 178-9, 187-8

Somali Coast.

(1) 1 January 1931; Official evaluation.

(2) to (5) *Year-Book League of Nations, 1932-3* to *1935-6*.

(7) Official evaluation: 1,362 Europeans and Assimilated (628 of European nationality, 499 Indians, 157 Abyssinians, 78 Jews); 68,420 Natives.

Somaliland (British).

(2) to (6) *Somaliland Blue Books, 1931-5*, Section 15, p. 2.

No census of the native population has ever been taken. It has been estimated in the *Blue Books* for a number of years at 344,700. *Statistical Abstract British Empire, 1926 to 1935*, p. 3, gives as total population for 1911, 1921, and 1931, 344,323, 347,000, and 344,700 respectively.

(7) *Non-Somali Census, April 26th 1931*, pp. 2, 9: 68 European and other white population; 520 East Indians (514 Natives of British India, 6 Natives of Portuguese India); 1,644 Coloured population (12 Persians, 1,614 Arabs, 11 Turks, 7 Egyptians); 451 Black population (100 Abyssinians, 89 Sudanese, 258 Natives of Nyasaland, 4 Swahilis). (According to *Colonial Report*, 1758, p. 6, the 1931 census showed '258 Nyasaland natives of the Somaliland Camel Corps', but according to the *Census Report*, 124 of the 258 Natives of Nyasaland were females.)

We have entered as Africans the 441 Blacks, the 7 Egyptians, and the Somalis (344,700).

The number of Whites in 1931-5 was 70, 70, 70, 76, and 68 respectively (*Blue Books, 1931-5*, Section 15, p. 2).

Birthplaces. Europeans, etc. (all of British nationality): 56 British Isles, 11 elsewhere in the British Empire, 1 elsewhere; East Indians: 195 British Somaliland, 82 Arabia, 234 British India, 6 Goa, 3 elsewhere; Coloured: 933 British Somaliland, 697 Arabia, 14 elsewhere; Black: 166 British Somaliland, 202 Nyasaland, 13 Sudan, 66 Abyssinia, 2 Arabia, 2 elsewhere. See *Census, 1931*, pp. 6-9.

Somaliland (Italian).

(1) 21 April 1931; *Annuario Statistico Italiano, 1936*, p. 264.

(2) to (5) *Year-Book League of Nations, 1932-3* to *1935-6*.

According to *Censimento Generale della Popolazione 21 Aprile 1931*, vol. V, pp. 44, 52, the population was composed as follows:

1,631 Italians; 37 Foreigners (Nationality: 36 European, 1 United States); 1,019,904 Natives.

Of the 1,668 non-Natives, 1,499 were born in Italy, 58 in Somaliland, 36 in other Italian colonies and possessions, 73 abroad, and 2 unknown (ibid., p. 49).

South West Africa.

(1) 3 May 1921; Territory of South-West Africa, *Report on the Census of the Population, 1921*, pp. v, 1. Enumerated population 106,429 (19,372 Europeans, 29,845 Mixed and Coloured, 57,212 Bantus). 'The following approximate figures of population in the areas which it was found impracticable to enumerate are more or less reliable: European 60, Mixed and coloured 1,000, Bantu 120,250.'

(2) to (5) *Report to the Council of the League of Nations concerning the Administration of South West Africa for the Year 1931*, p. 124; *1933*, p. 78; *1934*, pp. 95, 98; *Year Book of the Union of South Africa, 1934-5*, p. 1027. The figures for Europeans refer to 30 June. In *Statistical Abstract British Empire, 1924 to 1933*, p. 285, the total population is given as 240,520 for 1931 and as 239,900 for 31 December 1933 (apparently by omitting the large European population).

(6) 5 May 1936; *Year Book of the Union of South Africa, 1934-5*, p. 1,027. According to *Report to League, 1935*, pp. 82, 85, the total population in 1935 was estimated at 280,064.

(7) *Census, 1921*, p. 1: 19,432 Europeans; 177,462 Natives; 11 Asiatics; 30,834 Mixed and Other (for details of classification, see Chapter II).

(8) to (12) *Report to League, 1931*, p. 124; *1933*, p. 78; *1934*, pp. 95, 98; *1935*, pp. 82, 85.

(13) *Year Book of the Union of South Africa, 1934-5*, p. 1,027: 31,049 Europeans; 262,694 Bantus; 65,773 Other Coloured. These figures are subject to revision; *Census 1936, Preliminary Report*, p. i, gives: 30,505 Europeans; 69,546 Natives within the Police Zone; 14 Asiatics; 40,868 Mixed and Other.

(14) *Census, 1921*, pp. 15-16.

Spanish Guinea.

(1) 31 December 1920; *Censo de la Población de España, 1920*, vol. I, p. 336.

(2) to (5) *Year-Book League of Nations, 1932-3* to *1935-6*.

(6) *Almanach de Gotha, 1937*, p. 996.

The number of Whites is given in *Anuário Estadístico de España, 1934*, p. 18, as 1,539 (31 December 1930) and in *Almanach de Gotha, 1937*, p. 996, as 3,200.

Sudan (Anglo-Egyptian).

(2) *Sudan Almanac, 1933*, p. 40.

(3) to (6) Sudan Government, *Annual Report of the Secretary for Economic Development and Statistics of Foreign Trade, 1932-3*, p. 100; *1933-4*, p. 100; *1934*, p. 92; *1935*, p. 98. The race distribution is given as follows:

	1932	*31 Dec. 1933*	*31 Dec. 1934*	*31 Dec. 1935*
Natives of the Sudan ..	5,446,532	5,677,080	5,747,572	5,697,348
Indians	556	567	605	650
Egyptians	11,787	10,692	13,845	14,519
Europeans, Americans ..	5,947	5,341	6,419	6,776
Other non-Natives ..	43,103	34,871	47,935	48,525

Swaziland.

(1) 3 May 1921; Swaziland Administration, *Census of Swaziland, 1921*, p. 5. Natives: 'resident population (*de facto*),' 104,305; 'absentees at labour centres,' 5,990; 'total population (*de jure*),' 110,295.

(2) to (5) *Colonial Report*, 1594, p. 5; 1654, p. 5; 1694, p. 5; 1740, p. 5.

(6) 5 May 1936; Union of South Africa, *Census 1936, Preliminary Report*, p. i. In *Colonial Report*, 1793, p. 5, the population was estimated for 31 December 1935, at 127,355.

(7) to (13) *Census, 1921*, pp. 1, 14; *Colonial Report*, 1594, p. 5; 1654, p. 5; 1694, p. 5; 1740, p. 5; 1793, p. 5; *Census 1936, Preliminary Report*, p. i. For detailed classification, see Chapter II. The figures which we have entered as Africans include 444, 660, 680, 700, 720, 740, and 644 Coloured.

(14) *Census, 1921*, p. 14.

Tanganyika Territory (under British Mandate).

(1) 26 April 1931; *Census of the Native Population of Tanganyika Territory, 1931*, p. 10; *Report on the Non-Native Census in the Territory, 1931*, p. 10.

(2) to (6) Tanganyika Territory, *Blue Book for the Year ended 31st December 1931*, p. 108; *1932*, p. 111; *1933*, p. 120; *1934*, p. 121; *1935*, p. 126.

(7) *Census of the Native Population, 1931*, p. 10; *Non-Native Census, 1931*, pp. 10, 20-1: 8,228 Europeans; 23,422 Indians; 1,722 Goans; 7,059 Arabs; 178 Coloured; 30 Half-castes; 381 Other non-Natives; 5,022,640 Natives. We have counted as Asiatics the Indians, Goans, Arabs, and 'Other non-Natives'.

(8) to (12) *Blue Book, 1931*, p. 108; *1932*, p. 111; *1933*, p. 120; *1934*, p. 121; *1935*, p. 126. Population is subdivided into Europeans, Asiatics, and Natives.

(13) *Non-Native Census, 1931*, pp. 17-21.

Tangier.

(2) to (5) *Year-Book League of Nations, 1932-3* to *1935-6*.

(6) *Statesman's Year-Book, 1936*, p. 1,138.

The figure of 80,000 has been given for ten years in *Year-Book League of Nations*. Most recent estimates are lower:

Statesman's Year-Book, 1935, p. 1,127: About 51,000 (35,000 native Moslems, 11,000 Europeans, and 5,000 native Jews).

Statesman's Year-Book, 1936, p. 1,138: About 60,000 (36,500 native Moslems, 16,500 Europeans, and 7,000 native Jews).

Department of Overseas Trade, *Economic Conditions in Morocco, 1932-3*, p. 50: About 60,000 (40,000 native Mohammedans, 12,000 Europeans, and 8,000 native Jews).

L. Voinot, 'La question de Tanger,' *Questions Nord-Africaines*, No. 5, 15 April 1936, pp. 83-4: About 60,000 (35,000 native Moslems, 13,000 or 14,000 Europeans, and 11,000 Jews).

Togoland (under British Mandate).

(1) 26 April 1931; *The Gold Coast, 1931, Appendices*, p. 1.

(2) *Year-Book League of Nations, 1932-3*.

(3) (5) *Report to the Council of the League of Nations on the Administration of Togoland under British Mandate for the year 1932*, p. 64; *1934*, p. 51. Figures refer to 30 June.

(4) (6) *Statistical Abstract British Empire, 1924 to 1933*, p. 285; *1926 to 1935*, p. 303.

(7) *The Gold Coast, 1931, Appendices*, p. 1: 43 Non-Africans; 293,671 Africans.

The number of natives on 30 June 1932 to 1935 was 306,887, 317,461, 328,034, and 338,607 (*Report, 1932*, p. 64; *1933*, p. 55; *1934*, p. 51; *1935*, p. 55).

Togoland (under French Mandate).

(2) to (6) *Rapport annuel au Conseil de la Société des Nations sur l'administration sous mandat du territoire du Togo pour l'année 1931*, p. 84; *1932*, pp. 61-2; *1933*, p. 66; *1934*, p. 81; *1935*, p. 84.

(7) to (11) Ibid. The population is subdivided into Europeans, Syrians, and Natives.

Tunis.

(1) 22 March 1931; *Statistique générale de la Tunisie, 1931*, pp. 2-3. Civilian Population (exclusive of the Army of Occupation and of the Navy).

(2) to (5) *Year-Book League of Nations, 1932-3* to *1935-6*.

(6) Census 12 March 1936; *Statesman's Year-Book, 1937*, p. 913.

(7) *Statistique générale de la Tunisie, 1931*, pp. 2-7: (1) Europeans: 91,427 French (27,732 born in France, 48,334 in Tunis, 9,865 in Algeria, 352 in other French colonies and possessions, 5,144 in other countries); 103,866 Foreigners (91,178 Italians, 8,643 Maltese, 4,045 other Europeans); (2) Natives: 2,159,151 Moslems (2,086,762 Tunisians, 40,734 Algerians, 28,157 Tripolitans, 2,854 Moroccans, 445 Sudanese, 140 Syrians, 59 other nationalities); 56,248 Jews (55,340 Tunisians, 185 Algerians, 556 Tripolitans, 34 Moroccans, 28 Syrians, 105 other nationalities).

According to the preliminary results of the Census of 12 March 1936 (*Questions Nord-Africaines*, No. 7, 25 December 1936, p. 63), there were 213,205 Europeans: 108,068 French and 105,137 Foreigners (94,289 Italians, 7,279 Maltese, 3,569 other Europeans).

The French born in Tunis include a considerable number of non-Whites, especially naturalized native Jews and Moslems. From 1924 to 1931 altogether 19,886 naturalizations were granted, including 5,653 to Tunisian Jews and 76 to Algerian Jews (*Statistique générale de la Tunisie, 1931*, pp. 28-29; see also Julien Franc, 'La population de la Tunisie en 1931,' *Bulletin de la Société de Géographie d'Alger et de l'Afrique du Nord, 1932*, pp. 415-17). We have counted 90 per cent. of the 'Europeans' as Whites and 10 per cent. as Natives.

(8) *Statistique générale de la Tunisie, 1931*, pp. 6-8.

Uganda.

(1) 28 May 1931; Uganda Protectorate, *Census Returns, 1931*, p. 1.

(2) *Statistical Abstract British Empire, 1925 to 1931*, p. 3.

(3) to (6) Uganda Protectorate, *Blue Book, 1932*, p. 109; *1933*, p. 119; *1934*, p. 127; *1935*, p. 130.

(7) *Census Returns, 1931*, p. 1: 2,001 Europeans; 13,026 Indians; 1,124 Goans; 515 Arabs; 601 Others (non-Natives); 3,536,267 Natives. We have counted as Asiatics only the Indians, Goans. and Arabs. The 'Others' include an unknown number of Asiatics,

(8) to (11) *Blue Book, 1932*, p. 109; *1933*, p. 119; *1934*, p. 127; *1935*, p. 130. Population is subdivided into Whites, Asiatics (Indians, Goans), and Natives.

(12) *Census Returns, 1931*, pp. 35-8.

Zanzibar.

(1) 28 March 1931; Zanzibar Protectorate, *Report on the Census Enumeration of the Whole Population, 1931*, p. 1.

(2) *Statistical Abstract British Empire, 1925 to 1931*, p. 3.

(3) (4) (6) Zanzibar Protectorate, *Blue Book for the Year ended 31st December, 1932*, p. 78; *1933*, p. 84; *1935*, p. 86.

(5) *Colonial Report*, 1706, p. 6.

(7) *Census, 1931*, pp. 1-2: 278 Europeans; 33,401 Arabs; 14,242 British Indians; 1,004 Portuguese Indians; 37 Seychelles, Mauritians, Chinese, Japanese, and other non-Africans; 118,199 Local Africans; 68,267 Other (mainland) Africans. The number of persons returned as Arabs at the 1924 census was only 18,884. 'It appears from these figures that a certain proportion of Africans have returned themselves erroneously as Arabs.' We have counted as Asiatics the Indians and two-thirds of the Arabs.

North America

Alaska

(1) 1 October 1929; *Census of the United States, 1930, Outlying Territories and Possessions*, p. 3.

(2) to (6) *Statistical Abstract of the United States, 1936*, p. 10. Figures refer to 30 June. Population 30 June 1936: 62,000.

(7) *Census, 1930*, pp. 13, 15, 21: 28,640 Whites (pure-blooded); 29,983 Indians (22,155 full-blooded, 7,828 of mixed Indian and other blood); 26 Chinese; 278 Japanese; 136 Negroes; 164 Filipinos; 29 Mexicans; 11 Hawaiians; 11 Koreans.

Greenland.

(1) 1 October 1930; Danmarks Statistik, *Folketællingen i Grønland, 1930*, p. 33. Figure includes 271 inhabitants of Cape York.

(2) *International Yearbook of Agricultural Statistics, 1934-5*, p. 5.

(3) (5) *Year-Book League of Nations, 1933-4, 1935-6.*

(4) *Almanach de Gotha, 1937*, p. 826. Figure includes 269 inhabitants of Cape York.

(6) League of Nations, *Annual Epidemiological Report, 1935*, p. 65.

(7) *Folketællingen, 1930*, pp. 29, 33. Greenland proper: 408 Europeans; 16,222 Natives. Cape York: 5 Europeans; 266 Natives.

(8) *Almanach de Gotha, 1937*, p. 826. Greenland proper: 330 Europeans; 17,564 Natives ('Eskimoes and Half-castes'). Cape York: 4 Europeans; 265 Eskimoes.

(9) *Folketællingen, 1930*, p. 45; Greenland proper.

Labrador.

(1) 1921; *Statistical Abstract British Empire, 1926 to 1935*, p. 3.

(2) Ibid., p. 3.

(3) *Year-Book League of Nations, 1933-4.*

(4) (5) *Statesman's Year-Book, 1935*, p. 343; *1936*, p. 348.

(6) Census, August 1935; Newfoundland, *Annual Report of the Commission of Government for the year 1936*, p. 4.
'There are about 4,700 permanent inhabitants (some 750 Eskimo, the remainder of British descent).' (*Dominions Office and Colonial Office List, 1937*, p. 132.)

St. Pierre and Miquelon

(1) 1 July 1931; *Résultats statistiques du recensement, 1931*, vol. I, part I, p. 113.

(2) to (5) *Year-Book League of Nations, 1932-3* to *1935-6.*

(6) *Colonies Autonomes*, December 1935, p. 187.

(7) *Recensement, 1931*, vol. I, part I, p. 113: 4,067 French; 254 Foreigners.

Central America

Antigua.

(1) 24 April 1921; *Report on the Census of the Island of Antigua and its Dependencies, 1921*, p. 3.

(2) to (6) *Colonial Report*, 1607, p. 7; 1617, p. 5; 1704, p. 5; 1734, p. 5; 1782, p. 5.

(7) *Census, 1921*, p. 3: 914 White; 3,999 Coloured; 24,854 Black. There were 29,710 persons of European nationality, 39 Americans, 15 Syrians, and 3 Chinese (ibid., Table XI).

(8) *Census, 1921*, Table X.

Bahamas.

(1) 26 April 1931; *Report on the Census of the Bahama Islands, 1931*, p. 1.

(2) Bahamas, *Blue Book, 1932*, p. 162.

(3) to (6) *Colonial Report*, 1614, p. 6; 1661, p. 6; 1738, p. 6; 1768, p. 6.

'The total population is thus approximately 65,000, mostly of the African race. There is, however, a larger proportion of whites in the Bahamas than in any other West Indian Colony, many of them being descendants of soldiers who settled in the Bahamas after the War of American Independence' (*Colonial Report*, 1768, p. 6). Gilberto Loyo, *La Politica Demográfica de México*, Table following p. 485, México 1935, counts 16 per cent. for Whites and 42 per cent. each for Mulattos and Negroes.

(7) *Census, 1931*, p. 3.

Barbados.

(1) 24 April 1921; *Report on the Census of Barbados, 1921*, pp. 5-6. Figure includes 462 'Shipping' (population of ships at anchor), but excludes apparently 527 'Visitors to the Island'.

(2) to (6) *Colonial Report*, 1595, p. 6; 1632, p. 6; 1698, p. 5; 1725, p. 5; 1762, p. 6. Figures computed by adding to the census population of 1921 the excess of births over deaths and the excess of immigrants over emigrants. 'Estimates of population so calculated have usually been found to be exaggerated when a census is taken' (*Colonial Report*, 1762, p. 6).

(7) *Census, 1921*, pp. 21, 55: 10,748 White, 111,760 Black, 34,266 Mixed (including 319, 93, and 50 Shipping).

(8) *Census, 1921*, pp. 88-9. Of the 527 Visitors, 52 were born in Europe, 3 in Africa, 471 in America, and 1 in Asia (ibid., p. 54).

Bermuda.

(1) 17 May 1931; *Census of the Bermudas or Somers Islands, 1931*, Table No. 1; Bermuda, *Report of the Registrar General for the Year*

1931, p. 2. Figure includes 718 'Military including Civilians resident and employed on War Department Premises' and 666 'Naval employees'.

(2) to (6) *Report of the Registrar General*, *1931*, p. 2; 1932, p. 2; *1933*, p. 2; *1934*, p. 2; *1935*, p. 2. Figures represent 'Estimated Population for Statistical Purposes, including Military Population and Naval Personnel', i.e. 'Military resident in Bermuda' (330, 493, 488, 526, 539), 'Military Families resident in Bermuda' (67, 73, 69, 181, 61), and 'Naval employees, etc., as shewn in Census Report 1931' (666 in each year).

(7) *Report of the Registrar General*, *1931*, p. 2. 700 of the 718 'Military', and 653 of the 666 'Naval employees' were Whites.

(8) to (12) *Report of the Registrar General*, *1931*, p. 2; *1932*, p. 2; *1933*, p. 2; *1934*, p. 2; *1935*, p. 2. The civil population is subdivided into White and Coloured. We have assumed that the Military and their families were all white.

British Honduras.

(1) 26 April 1931; *Census of British Honduras*, *1931*, p. 3.

(2) to (6) *Colonial Report*, 1610, p. 6; 1647, p. 6; 1690, p. 6; 1713, p. 6; 1764, p. 6.

'The total number of residents of unblemished white stock is certainly not in excess of 200, men, women, and children' (*South American Handbook*, *1936*, p. 218). According to *Almanch de Gotha*, *1936*, p. 965: about 600 Europeans; 200 North Americans; and 2,000 Creoles.

(7) *Census*, *1931*, pp. 40-7.

Cayman Islands.

(1) 25 April 1921; *Census of Jamaica and its Dependencies*, *1921*, p. 71.

(2) *Colonial Report*, 1575, p. 7.

(3) *Year-Book League of Nations*, *1933-34*.

(4) (6) *Statistical Abstract British Empire*, *1924 to 1933*, p. 4; *1926 to 1935*, p. 4.

(5) *Statesman's Year-Book*, *1935*, p. 351. According to census of 7 August 1934, 6,009 (*Colonial Report*, 1745, p. 8).

(7) *Census of Jamaica*, *1921*, p. 72: 1,994 White; 2,431 Coloured; 828 Black. 'A large percentage of those returned as whites are octoroons, or even darker in complexion. The number of persons

of unmixed Caucasian blood is relatively small. There is a very negligible admixture of Indian blood.'

(8) *Colonial Report*, 1745, p. 8: 2,368 White; 840 Black; 2,797 Coloured; 2 East Indian; 2 Carib.

(9) *Census of Jamaica, 1921*, p. 73. Birthplaces are given only for British subjects. We have entered the 43 foreigners (nationality: 28 United States, 1 Cuban, 6 Nicaraguan, 2 Honduran, 2 Columbian, 1 Swedish, 2 Norwegian, 1 Danish) under 'Others'.

Curaçao

(1) 31 December 1911; *Year-Book League of Nations, 1935-6*; *Jaarcijfers voor het Koninkrijk der Nederlanden, Koloniën, 1921*, p. 154.

(2) to (5) *Statistical Annual of Curaçao for the Year 1934*, p. 3.

(6) *Almanach de Gotha, 1937*, p. 1193.

According to Hübners *Geographisch-statistische Tabellen, 1929*, p. 250, in 1926: 55,000 Black; 1,200 Europeans; 1,600 other Foreigners. Loyo counts 7·2 per cent. for White and 92·8 for Negro.

Dominica.

(1) 24 April 1921; Dominica, *Census, 1921, Report by the Registrar-General*, p. iv.

(2) to (6) *Colonial Report*, 1607, p. 36; 1617, p. 5; 1704, p. 5; 1734, p. 5; 1782, p. 5.

(7) *Census, 1921*, pp. vi-vii: 556 White; 11,563 Coloured (including 141 pure blooded Caribs); 24,940 Black.

(8) *Census, 1921*, p. 6.

Grenada.

(1) 24 April 1921; Grenada, *Report and General Abstracts of the Census of 1921*, p. 1.

(2) to (6) *Colonial Report*, 1789, p. 5.

(7) *Census, 1921*, p. 10: 905 White; 11,673 Mixed; 51,032 Black; 2,692 Oriental; but 'the "Whites" may safely be reduced by about 10 per cent. and the "Mixed" correspondingly increased'. We have changed the original figures accordingly.

(8) *Census, 1921*, p. 52.

Guadeloupe.

(1) 1 July 1931; *Bulletin de l'agence générale des colonies 1932*, pp. 666-7.

(2) to (5) *Year-Book League of Nations, 1932-3* to *1935-6*. According to *Almanach de Gotha*, 1936, p. 1,114: 8 per cent. Creoles; 65 per cent. Mulattos; 27 per cent. Negroes.

Jamaica.

(1) 25 April 1921; *Census of Jamaica and its Dependencies, 1921*, p. 1.

(2) to (6) *Colonial Report*, 1603, p. 5; 1653, p. 5; 1686, p. 5; 1730, p. 5; 1796, p. 5.

(7) *Census, 1921*, p. 7: 14,476 White; 157,223 Coloured; 660,420 Black; 18,610 East Indians; 3,696 Chinese; 3,693 Not Specified.

(8) *Census, 1921*, pp. 52-5, 61. East Indians born in Jamaica 11,349, in India 7,103, Elsewhere 35, Not Stated 123.

Martinique.

(1) 1 July 1931; *Résultats statistiques du recensement général, 1931*, vol. I, part I, p. 113. According to *Bulletin de l'agence générale des colonies, 1932*, p. 662: 232,355; according to *Statesman's Year-Book, 1936*, p. 947: 234,695.

(2) (3) *Year-Book League of Nations, 1932-3, 1933-4*.

(4) *Bulletin de l'agence économique des colonies, 1934*, p. 923.

(5) *Revue d'histoire des colonies, 1935, Memento Colonial*, p. 146: 239,296 *sédentaires*; 5,123 from the mother country; 489 foreign Europeans.

(6) League of Nations, *Annual Epidemiological Report, 1935*, p. 65; *Statesman's Year-Book, 1937*, p. 914.

'The inhabitants are mainly Negroes and Mulattos, 15,000 Indians and Chinese, 5,000 Whites' (*Almanach de Gotha, 1936*, p. 1,114). Hübners *Geographisch-statistische Tabellen, 1936*, p. 228, gives an estimate of 10,000 Whites. Loyo counts 4·2 per cent. as White; 44·7 as Mulatto; 44·8 as Negro; and 6·3 as Asiatic.

Montserrat.

(1) 24 April 1921; Montserrat, *Census Report, 1921*, p. 3.

(2) to (6) *Colonial Report*, 1607, p. 49; 1617, p. 5; 1704, p. 5; 1734, p. 5; 1782, p. 5.

(7) *Colonial Report*, 1734, p. 5: 112 White; 2,503 Coloured; 9,505 Black.

(8) to (11) Leeward Islands, *Blue Books, 1932-5*, Section 15, p. 5. Population subdivided into White and Coloured.

(12) *Census Report, 1921*, p. 9.

Panama Canal Zone.

(1) 1 April 1930; *Census of the United States, 1930, Outlying Territories and Possessions*, pp. 325, 328. Civilian population, 27,682; Military and Naval population (all inhabitants residing on military or naval reservations), 11,875.

(2) to (5) *Year-Book League of Nations, 1932-3* to *1935-6*. Population 30 June 1931 to 1934: 41,500, 43,100, 44,700, 46,400 (*Statistical Abstract of the United States, 1934*, p. 10); Civilian population 30 June 1935, 29,636 (*Statesman's Year-Book, 1936*, p. 1,202).

(6) *Almanach de Gotha, 1937*, p. 728: 1936, civilian population 29,190, garrison 12,000.

(7) *Census, 1930*, p. 328: 18,814 Whites; 20,385 Negroes; 268 Other Coloured (34 Indians, 88 Chinese, 85 Hindus, 37 Filipinos, 24 Others). Civilian population: 7,373 Whites; 20,113 Negroes; 196 Other Coloured. Military and naval population: 11,441 Whites; 272 Negroes; 72 Other Coloured.

Puerto Rico.

(1) 1 April 1930; *Census of the United States, 1930, Outlying Territories and Possessions*, p. 123.

(2) to (5) *Statistical Abstract of the United States, 1936*, p. 10. Figures refer to mid-year.

(6) 1 December 1935; ibid., p. 40. Mid-year 1935 and 1936: 1,710,300 and 1,742,000 (ibid., p. 10).

(7) *Census, 1930*, pp. 133, 136: 'The divisions of the population by color or race are: White; colored (comprising Negroes and persons of mixed white and Negro blood); and other races' (2 Mexicans, 5 Indians, 23 Chinese, 6 Japanese, 2 Filipinos).

The classification by country of birth (see ibid., pp. 145-6) does not permit showing the distribution by continent of birth, but it appears that of the total population of 1,543,913, no less than 1,534,535 were born in Puerto Rico.

St. Kitts and Nevis.

(1) 24 April 1921; Leeward Islands, *St. Kitts-Nevis, Census Report, 1921*, p. 2.

(2) to (6) *Colonial Report*, 1607, p. 20; 1617, p. 5; 1704, p. 5; 1734, p. 5; 1782, p. 5.

(7) *Census Report, 1921*, p. 2: 1,219 White; 6,204 Coloured; 30,791 Black. 'The population of these islands can be roughly divided into three classes—viz., those of pure European extraction numbering about three to four hundred, the educated coloured class numbering about 7,000, and the labouring class, white, coloured and black about 28,583' (*Colonial Report*, 1607, p. 20). We have counted as Asiatics 23 persons born in India and 13 others listed as Asiatics.

(8) *Census Report, 1921*, Table No. 12.

St. Lucia.

(1) 24 April 1921; *Report on the Census of the Colony of Saint Lucia, 1921*, pp. 1, 4. Figure includes 55 Shipping.

(2) to (6) *Colonial Report*, 1648, p. 5; 1693, p. 5; 1761, p. 5. Resident population.

(7) *Census, 1921*, pp. 6, 8, 34-35.

St. Vincent.

(1) 26 April 1931; *Saint Vincent, Report and General Abstracts of the Census of 1931*, p. 2.

(2) *Almanach de Gotha, 1937*, p. 909.

(3) to (6) *Colonial Report*, 1676, p. 4; 1759, p. 4.

(7) *Census, 1931*, p. 24: 33,257 Negroes; 11,292 Coloured; 2,107 'Whites'; 66 'Europeans'; 1,239 Others. We have counted as Asiatics 628 persons born in St. Vincent of East Indian parents and 25 persons born in India.

(8) *Census, 1931*, pp. 7, 22.

Trinidad and Tobago.

(1) 26 April 1931; *Census of the Colony of Trinidad and Tobago, 1931*, pp. 6-7. Figure includes 1,089 afloat.

(2) to (6) *Colonial Report*, 1634, p. 7; 1720, p. 7; 1767, p. 7.

(7) *Census, 1931*, pp. 6, 15, 26, 31: (*a*) 'General population (that is the population excluding the East Indians)', 274,116; (*b*) East Indians, 138,667. The General Population comprised mainly Negroes, Mulattos, Whites, and the Chinese Colony (2,027 born in China, 2,054 'born locally of Chinese Parents,' 1,108 'born

locally of Chinese Fathers only,' 50 'born locally of Chinese Mothers only'), and Syrians. The East Indians included 1,713 born in Trinidad 'of Indian father only,' and 805 born in Trinidad 'of Indian mother only'. We have allocated 15 per cent. of the General Population to Whites, 83 per cent. to Africans, and 2 per cent. to Asiatics.

(8) *Census, 1931*, pp. 16A, 26, 31.

Turks and Caicos Islands.

(1) 25 April 1921; *Census of Jamaica and its Dependencies, 1921*, p. 65. Figure includes 34 foreigners on board vessels.

(2) (3) (5) *Colonial Report*, 1582, p. 4; 1636, p. 4; 1733, p. 4.

(6) *Statistical Abstract British Empire, 1926 to 1935*, p. 4.

(7) *Census, 1921*, p. 69: 210 White; 1,503 Coloured; 3,900 Black.

(8) *Colonial Report*, 1733, p. 4: 'It is estimated that of the whole population, 5,140 or 97 per cent. were "coloured" (of mixed descent), while 160 or 3 per cent. were "white."'

The birthplaces are given as follows (*Census, 1921*, p. 70): Turks and Caicos Islands 5,406, United Kingdom 7, Canada 28, other British Colonies 65, United States of America 25, Haiti 35, San Domingo 38, various 8.

Virgin Islands (British).

(1) 25 April 1921; Registrar General, *Table showing the Number of Inhabitants, etc., in the Presidency of the Virgin Islands according to the Census of 25th April, 1921.*

(2) to (6) *Colonial Report*, 1607, p. 60; 1617, p. 5; 1704, p. 5; 1734, p. 5; 1782, p. 5.

(7) *Table Census, 1921:* 36 White; 1,158 Coloured; 3,888 Black.

(8) Leeward Islands, *Blue Book, 1932*, Section 15, p. 5: 22 White; 5,187 Coloured.

Virgin Islands (U.S.A.).

(1) 1 April 1930; *Census of the United States, 1930, Outlying Territories and Possessions*, p. 259.

(2) to (5) *Year-Book League of Nations, 1932-3 to 1935-6.*

(7) *Census, 1930*, pp. 261, 264: 2,010 Whites; 17,243 Negroes; 2,719 Mixed (those of a mixture of White and Negro); 4 Filipinos; 1 Indian; 17 Chinese; 18 Hindus.

(8) *Census, 1930*, pp. 270-1.

South America

British Guiana.

(1) 26 April 1931; British Guiana, *Report on the Results of the Census of the Population, 1931*, pp. iv-vi. Figure includes 7,379 'Aboriginal Indians living in their primitive state in the remote parts of the Colony.'

(2) to (6) *Colonial Report*, 1598, p. 7; 1644, p. 7; 1692, p. 7; 1728, p. 7; 1765, p. 7.

(7) *Census, 1931*, pp. 120-1.

(8) to (12) *Colonial Report*, 1598, p. 7; 1644, p. 7; 1692, p. 7; 1728, p. 7; 1765, p. 7.

The race distribution was as follows:

	26 April 1931	*31 Dec. 1931*	*31 Dec. 1932*	*31 Dec. 1933*	*31 Dec. 1934*	*31 Dec. 1935*
Europeans, other than Portuguese	2,127	2,085	2,078	2,051	2,039	2,186
Portuguese	8,612	8,641	8,654	8,625	8,546	8,503
East Indians	130,540	131,919	134,059	135,114	136,004	138,334
Chinese	2,951	3,019	3,015	3,109	3,099	3,241
Blacks	124,203[1]	124,838	126,077	127,103	127,301	128,559
Aborigines[2]	8,348	8,365	8,430	8,557	8,601	8,723
Mixed Races	33,800	34,404	35,159	36,368	37,278	38,352
Not Stated	352	348	341	333	303	321

[1] Including 67 'Africans' born in Africa.

[2] Only Aborigines in the settled areas.

We have counted the 'Portuguese', the Blacks, and the Mixed races as Africans.

(13) *Census, 1931*, pp. xxx, 124-5, 150-1:

Race	*Born in Colony*	*Born elsewhere*
Europeans, other than Portuguese	1,058	1,069
Portuguese	7,939	673
East Indians	106,453	24,087 (23,236 in India)
Chinese	2,528	423 (in China)
Africans	—	67 (in Africa)
Blacks	116,709	7,427 (in West Indies)
Aborigines	8,348	—
Mixed Races	31,617	2,183 (in West Indies)
Races not stated	—	352

Falkland Islands and Dependencies.

(1) 26 April 1931; Falkland Islands, *Report of Census, 1931*, p. 2.

(2) (4) (6) *Statistical Abstract British Empire, 1925 to 1931*, p. 4; *1924 to 1933*, p. 4; *1926 to 1935*, p. 4.

(3) (5) Falkland Islands, *Annual Medical and Sanitary Report, 1932*, p. 3; *1934*, p. 3.

'The inhabitants of the Falkland Islands are of European, chiefly British, descent, Scotch blood being marked. There is no indigenous or native population' (*Colonial Report*, 1788, p. 5). 'The British inhabitants of South Georgia are limited practically to the Government staff and to the crews of British vessels. The remainder are almost exclusively Norwegian or Scandinavian' (Ibid., p. 21).

On 24 April 1921, the distribution by birthplace was in Falkland Islands: Europe 448 (of whom 414 in Great Britain), Africa 2, America 1639, Asia 1, Oceania 4, At Sea 1; in South Georgia (including shipping): Europe 1,279 (of whom 149 in Great Britain, 830 in Norway, 157 in Sweden), Cape Verde Islands 51, America 7 (Falkland Islands, *Report of Census, 1921*, p. 12).

On 26 April 1931, the distribution by birthplace was in Falkland Islands: Europe 397 (of whom 363 in United Kingdom), Africa 2, America 1,983, Asia 2, Oceania 7, At Sea 1 (*Census, 1931*, p. 13).

French Guiana, Inini Territory.

(1) 1 July 1931. The published data are quite contradictory. *Résultats statistiques du recensement général*, vol. I, part I, p. 113, gives 28,310 Europeans and Assimilated (including 5,419 convicts), 1,000 Natives. *Bulletin de l'agence générale des colonies, 1932*, pp. 668-9, gives for French Guiana 22,169 (17,944 French, 2,934 Foreigners, 1,240 Liberated convicts, 51 Relegated) and for Inini Territory 3,511 (983 French, 1,319 Foreigners, 441 Native Tribes, 767 gold seekers, etc.). *Colonies Autonomes*, December 1935, p. 173, gives the same totals, but adds: 'These figures do not include the aboriginal Indians of the interior who have fled from civilization.' *Statesman's Year-Book, 1936*, p. 947, says that the figure of 22,169 (the author erroneously believes it to include Inini Territory) is 'exclusive of the population of the penal settlement of Maroni, of the floating population of miners without any fixed abode, as also of officials, troops, and native tribes. . . . The military force consists of 310 officers and men of the Colonial Infantry. . . . In 1931 the penal population consisted of 5,954 men'. *South American Handbook, 1937*, p. 367, states: 'The population, inclusive

of natives, is estimated at 25,679.' Hübners *Geographisch-statistische Tabellen, 1936*, p. 228, gives as population 25,679, and 'with wild natives' 45,679. *Almanach de Gotha, 1937*, p. 1,052, gives as population 32,596. We have accepted the latter figure.

(2) to (5) *Year-Book League of Nations, 1932-3* to *1935-6.*

Surinam.

(2) to (4) *Surinam Report, 1933, II Statistical Abstract*, p. 3; ibid., *1934, II*, p. 3.

(5) *Statistical Annual of Surinam for the Year 1934*, p. 3.

(6) *Almanach de Gotha, 1937*, p. 1,192.

(7) to (11) *Report, 1932, II*, p. 4; *1933, II*, p. 4; *1934, II*, pp. 3-4; *Statistical Annual, 1934*, pp. 3-4; *Almanach de Gotha, 1937*, p. 1,192.

	31 Dec. 1931	*31 Dec. 1932*	*31 Dec. 1933*	*31 Dec. 1934*	*31 Dec. 1935*
Europeans	1,725	1,798	1,858	1,886	1,938
Natives	60,764	61,658	62,679	63,982	65,186
Netherlands-Indians	31,502	32,257	32,922	33,560	33,386
British Indians ..	36,756	37,420	38,333	39,393	40,777
Chinese	1,845	1,907	2,009	2,014	2,076
Others	3,626	3,654	3,707	3,550	3,480
Bush Negroes ..	17,242	17,000	17,000	17,000	17,000
Aboriginal Indians ..	2,428	2,500	2,700	2,700	2,500

Asia

Aden and Perim.

(1) 26 February 1931; *Census of India, 1931*, vol. VIII, part III, p. 4.

(2) to (5) *Year-Book League of Nations, 1932-3* to *1935-6.*

According to *Census, 1931*, vol. VIII, part III, pp. 14-5: 275 Europeans; 31,303 Arabs; 4,046 Somalis; 7,362 Indians; 4,150 Jews; 773 Military; 429 Miscellaneous (Anglo-Indians, Chinese, Native Christians, etc.); Grand Total 48,338. 'In this statement the population of the Ports of Aden and Perim is not included.' The 'Total Military' was 1,981 (see ibid., p. 4).

(7) *Census, 1931*, vol. VIII, part III, p. 17.

Aegean Islands.

(1) 21 April 1931; *Annuario Statistico Italiano, 1936*, p. 250.

(2) to (6) *Annuario, 1933*, p. 453; *1934*, p. 250; *1936*, p. 266. Population 21 April 1936 (Census) 140,729 (*Notiziario demografico, 1937*, pp. 87-8).

According to *Censimento Generale della Popolazione, 21 Aprile 1931*, vol. V, pp. 56, 66, the population was composed as follows: 5,866 Italians; 6,863 Foreigners (nationality: 3,189 Greece, 419 other European nationality, 2,308 Turkey, 5 Persia, 227 Egypt, 3 Argentine, 1 Bolivia, 14 Uruguay, 537 United States, 48 Australia, 112 Stateless); 118,113 Dodecanesans.

Of the 5,866 Italians, 3,571 were born in Italy, 1,173 on the Aegean Islands, 12 in other Italian colonies and possessions, 1,107 abroad, and 3 unknown (ibid., p. 63).

According to *Notiziario demografico, 1937*, pp. 87-8, there were on 21 April 1936 on the Aegean Islands 16,711 Italians (increase due in part to concentration of troops during the war against Ethiopia); 4,114 Foreigners; 119,904 Dodecanesans.

Brunei.

(1) 1 April 1931; British Malaya, *A Report on the 1931 Census and on Certain Problems of Vital Statistics*, pp. 120-1.

(2) *Statistical Abstract British Empire, 1925 to 1931*, p. 4.

(3) to (6) State of Brunei, *Annual Report of the Medical Department, 1935*, p. 13.

(7) *Report on the 1931 Census*, pp. 120-1, 201: 60 Europeans; 10 Eurasians; 25,670 Malays (Malaysians, excluding aboriginals, who belong to British Malaya); 1,302 other Malaysians; 2,683 Chinese; 377 Indians; 33 Others (12 Arabs, 7 Ceylon Peoples, 2 Filipinos, 8 Japanese, 4 Others).

According to *Colonial Report*, 1624, p. 3, 1662, p. 7, 1751, p. 7, 1753, p. 7, the distribution by race was as follows:

	31 Dec. 1932	*31 Dec. 1933*	*31 Dec. 1934*	*31 Dec. 1935*
Europeans	60	90	84	84
Eurasians	10	30	32	40
Malaysians	27,000	28,000	28,000	28,800
Chinese	3,000	4,280	4,000	4,000
Indians	220	200	200	200
Others	300	300	655	608

(8) *Report on the 1931 Census*, p. 215. Birthplace of Europeans: Great Britain and Ireland 41, Canada 2, Elsewhere in British Empire 8, United States of America 6, Holland 1, Elsewhere outside British Empire 2. We have counted those born 'elsewhere in British Empire' as born in Asia and those born 'elsewhere outside British Empire' as born in Europe.

Ceylon.

(1) 26 February 1931; *Census Publications, Ceylon, 1931*, vol. I, p. 1.

(2) to (6) *Report of the Registrar-General of Ceylon for 1931*, p. 5; *1932*, p. 5; *1933* p. 5,; *1934*, p. 5; *1935*, p. 5. Totals exclude military and shipping (Census 1931: 1,387 and 4,290 respectively). The decrease in 1935 was due to the malaria epidemic.

(7) *Census Publications, Ceylon, 1921*. vol. I, part I, p. 191.

(8) to (12) *Report of the Registrar-General of Ceylon for 1932*, p. 29; *1933*, p. 29; *1934*, p. 33; *1935*, p. 31.

Date	*Europeans*	*Eurasians*	*Sinhalese, Tamils, Moors*	*Malays*	*Others*	*Total*
18 March 1921 (*a*) ..	8,937	29,532	4,423,553	13,461	24,556	4,504,549[1]
18 March 1921 (*b*) ..	8,118	29,439	4,421,177	13,402	21,959	4,498,605[1]
26 February 1931 (*b*) ..	9,153	32,315	5,216,420	15,977	32,564	5,306,871[2]
1 July 1932 (*b*) ..	9,700	35,200	5,293,400	16,100	31,700	5,386,100
1 July 1933 (*b*) ..	9,800	35,400	5,322,300	16,100	31,900	5,415,500
1 July 1934 (*b*) ..	10,000	36,300	5,456,100	16,500	32,700	5,551,600
1 July 1935 (*b*) ..	10,100	36,600	5,502,100	16,700	33,000	5,598,500

(*a*) Total population. (*b*) Population excluding Military and Shipping.
[1] Including 4,510 Veddas.
[2] Including 442 persons of unspecified race.

The figures for 18 March 1921 are census results. For 26 February 1931, the total population was enumerated, but the race distribution was ascertained only in the Colombo Municipality (287,729) and on the estates (790,376), and was estimated for the rest of the Island on the basis of the Census of 1921. The figures for 1932-5 are estimates.

According to the Census report of 1921 (vol. I, part I, pp. 192, 214), a number of Eurasians were returned as Europeans. 'The majority of the [21,959] persons enumerated as "Others" were Indians (20,303) of various races, while among the rest were Afghans (304), Africans (24), Arabs (227), Armenians (1), Baluchis (164), Boers (1), Burmese (115), Chilians (1), Chinese (104), East Indians (13), Egyptians (6), Filipinos (4), Japanese (42), Javanese (14), Jews (4), Kaffirs (255), Lacadivians (1), Madagascarians (3), Maldivians (30), Mauritians (16), Persians (14), Siamese (13), Somalis (6), Syrians (20),

Turks (3), West Indians (3), and other Asiatics (61). The following races of European descent, which could not strictly be classified as Europeans, were included under "Others": Americans (105), Australians (80), Canadians (12).' (Ibid., p. 228.) An analysis of the detailed table on the population by individual races (vol. IV, pp. 32-7) leads us to the conclusion that 'Others' included in addition 8 New Zealanders and 2 Mongolians.

We have allocated 200 of those counted as Europeans to Asiatics (Eurasians). Of those counted as 'Others' we have allocated 200 to Whites, 300 to Africans, and the rest to Asiatics.

(13) *Census Publications, Ceylon, 1921*, vol. IV, pp. 164-6. Figures exclude Military and Shipping.

Cyprus.

(1) 27 April 1931; *Report and General Abstracts of the Census of 1931*, p. 1. Total includes Military (151).

(2) to (6) *Colonial Report*, 1574, p. 6; 1618, p. 5; 1663, p. 6; 1741, p. 6; 1778, p. 6.

(7) *Report Census, 1931*, pp. 19, 65-6. Of the 4,635 persons recorded as born in Europe, 2,940 are recorded as born in 'Turkey'. We have assumed that their birthplace was actually in Europe since 1,589 other persons are recorded as born in 'Asia Minor'.

Federated Malay States.

(1) 1 April 1931; British Malaya, *Report on the 1931 Census*, pp. 120-1, 127. Figure includes 423 'population enumerated on Sea-going Ships', but excludes all persons enumerated on the railway (total for British Malaya, 1,496).

(2) *Statistical Abstract British Empire, 1925 to 1931*, p. 4.

(3) (4) *Year-Book League of Nations, 1933-4, 1934-5*. Population on 30 June 1931 to 1936: 1,723,117, 1,622,903, 1,597,770, 1,631,728, 1,777,421, 1,847,951; see *Report of the Registrar-General of Births and Deaths, 1931*, p. 1; *1932*, p. 1; *1933*, p. 1; *1934*, p. 1; *1935*, p. 2; *Dominions Office and Colonial Office List, 1937*, p. 384.

(5) (6) *Report of the Registrar-General, 1934*, p. 2; *1935*, p. 2.

(7) *Report on the 1931 Census*, pp. 120-1, 165, 200: 6,350 Europeans (including 102 Dutch, 104 French, and 20 Portuguese, who in part are Half-castes); 4,251 Eurasians; 443,618 Malays (see Brunei); 150,113 other Malaysians; 711,540 Chinese; 379,996 Indians; 17,228 Others (19 Annamese, 402 Arabs, 15 Armenians, 13,648 Ceylon

Peoples, 290 Filipinos, 1,323 Japanese, 10 Jews, 4 Negroes, 20 Persians, 1,435 Siamese, 62 Others). Figures do not include 423 on Sea-going Ships.

According to *Report of the Registrar-General, 1932*, p. 1, *1933*, p. 1, *1934*, p. 1, *1935*, p. 2, and *Dominions Office and Colonial Office List, 1937*, p. 384, the distribution by race was as follows:

	30 June 1932	*30 June 1933*	*30 June 1934*	*30 June 1935*	*31 Dec. 1935*	*30 June 1936*
Malaysians	605,521	615,651	627,461	643,003	649,414	657,657
Chinese ..	665,206	644,120	653,977	717,614	737,440	761,077
Indians ..	324,796	310,752	322,089	387,917	397,582	400,080
Europeans	5,959	5,988	6,504	7,145	7,617	8,165
Eurasians ..	21,431	21,259	21,697	4,581	4,635	4,696
Others ..				17,161	17,026	16,276

(8) *Report on the 1931 Census*, p. 213. Birthplace of Europeans: Great Britain and Ireland 3,892, Australia 461, New Zealand 131, Canada 20, British Malaya 931, Elsewhere in British Empire 391, United States of America 115, Denmark 58, France 106, Germany 19, Holland 15, Netherlands East Indies 21, Elsewhere outside British Empire 188, Not Stated 2. We have counted those born ' elsewhere in British Empire ' as born in Asia and those born ' elsewhere outside British Empire ' as born in Europe.

Formosa (including Pescadores Islands).

(1) 1 October 1930; *Résumé statistique de l'Empire du Japon*, vol. 50, p. 4.

(2) to (5) Ibid., p. 6.

(6) 1 October 1935 (Census); ibid., p. 4.

The figures do not include the officers and privates of the Army and Navy residing in Formosa; see *Financial and Economic Annual of Japan, 1935*, p. 2.

According to *Résumé*, vol. 50, p. 6, the figures include all aborigines; according to *Financial and Economic Annual, 1935*, p. 2, they ' include the Formosan aborigines living in the administrative territories, but do not include the aborigines of the interior '; according to Tsuneta Yano and Kyoichi Shirasaki, *Nippon, A Chartered Survey of Japan, 1936*, p. 451, 90,000 aborigines ' outside the normal administrative area ' are not included in the official figures.

(7) (8) *Japan-Manchoukuo Year Book, 1936*, p. 529; *1937*, p. 539. The race distribution is given as follows (for 1931-2, see *Résumé*

statistique, vol. 50, p. 6; for 1935 *Nippon Yusen Kaisha's Official Guide, Glimpses of the East, 1936-7*, Taiwan, p. 3):

	1 Oct. 1930	*31 Dec. 1931*	*31 Dec. 1932*	*31 Dec. 1933*	*31 Dec. 1934*	*1 Oct. 1935*
Japanese	232,299	243,872	248,539	256,327	262,964	271,922
Koreans				1,191	1,316	
Natives	4,313,922	4,514,820	4,641,686	4,759,197	4,882,288	4,883,857
Chinese	46,691	45,284	42,208	43,585	48,193	57,039
Other Foreigners ..				207	219	

We have entered the 'Other Foreigners' as Whites.

French India.

(1) 1 July 1931; Statistique générale de la France, *Résultats statistiques du recensement, 1931*, vol. I, part I, p. 116.

(2) *Year-Book League of Nations, 1932-3.*

(3) (4) *Bulletin de l'agence économique des colonies, 1934*, p. 1,240.

(5) *International Yearbook of Agricultural Statistics, 1934-5*, p. 9.

(6) *Statesman's Year-Book, 1937*, p. 915.

(7) *Résultats statistiques du recensement, 1931*, vol. I, part I, p. 116: 236,539 French; 49,871 Foreigners. *Bulletin de l'agence générale des colonies, 1932*, pp. 1869-70: (1) Europeans: 427 French (persons born in France or born in French India of parents who came from France or from other French colonies); 691 'Descendants of Europeans or Creoles' (Half-castes of European habits); 417 Foreigners; (2) Half-castes: 842 French; 210 Foreigners; (3) Natives: 232,493 French; 49,296 Foreigners. We have counted as Whites the French Europeans and three-quarters of the Foreign Europeans.

French Indo-China.

(1) 1 July 1931; *Résultats statistiques du recensement, 1931*, vol. I, part I, p. 116; *Bulletin de la Statistique générale de la France*, January-March 1937, p. 284. Figure includes 32,300 Military.

(2) to (5) *Year-Book League of Nations, 1932-3* to *1935-6.*

(6) Census, 1 July 1936; *Bulletin de la Statistique*, January-March 1937, p. 284; *La Revue du Pacifique, 1937*, p. 54. Figure includes 30,469 Military.

(7) *Résultats statistiques du recensement, 1931*, vol. I, part I, pp. 113, 116; *Annuaire statistique de l'Indochine, 1931-2*, p. 55: (1) Europeans and Assimilated ('persons of European status; including the French of the old colonies, the European half-castes,

the naturalized Natives, the Japanese, the Filipinos'): 39,821 French (including 12,081 Military); 1,665 Foreigners; (2) Natives: 20,962,000 French subjects and French protected persons; 428,000 Foreigners of special status (418,000 Chinese, 10,000 Hindus and others); 20,000 Military. According to *Annuaire statistique de l'Indochine, 1931-2*, p. 56, *1932-3*, p. 49, the 'European' population (persons of European status) was as follows:

	31 Dec. 1931	*31 Dec. 1932*	*31 Dec. 1933*
French civilians ..	30,476	34,813	33,501
Foreign civilians ..	1,219	1,256	1,121
Military and sailors ..	12,144	10,849	11,320
Total	43,839	46,918	45,942

(8) *Bulletin de la Statistique*, January-March 1937, p. 284; *La Géographie, 1937*, p. 104; *La Revue du Pacifique, 1937*, p. 54: (1) Persons of European status: 30,711 French civilians; 975 Foreign civilians (including Japanese and Filipinos); 10,574 Military and Sailors; (2) Natives: 22,637,000 French subjects and French protected persons; 325,800 Foreigners of privileged status (Chinese); 5,400 Foreigners of special status (Indians, British subjects, Siamese, Javanese); 19,895 Military and Sailors.

We have counted three-quarters of the persons of European status as Whites.

Hong Kong.

(1) 7 March 1931; *Report on the Census of the Colony of Hong Kong, 1931*, p. 15. Includes 68,721 Chinese afloat. 'As regards the population afloat normally based on Hong Kong . . . the figures obtained are less than what would be expected. The fishing fleet and large cargo boats had been in port over Chinese New Year's Day, the crews had had their holiday, had probably spent all their money and they were off again to earn more. They were conspicuously absent on Census Night.'

(2) to (6) *Colonial Report*, 1585, p. 5; 1637, p. 4; 1673, p. 5; 1712, p. 4; 1775, p. 4. Figures refer to middle of year; Defence forces (7 March 1931, 8,953) excluded; Chinese afloat ('in junks and sampans') estimated at 100,000. Civilian population, 30 June 1936, 988,190 (*Dominions Office and Colonial Office List, 1937*, p. 320).

(7) *Report on the Census, 1931*, pp. 25-7: 821,429 Chinese; 16,402 'Europeans' (14,366 British races including 7,683 Defence

Forces, 2,036 other European races and U.S.A.); 837 Eurasians; 3,197 Local Portuguese (' that is, those born in Hong Kong, Macao or China); 4,745 Indians including 1,270 Defence Forces; 2,205 Japanese; 936 Others (338 Filipinos, 241 Malays, 235 other Asiatics, 16 Cubans, 6 Hawaiians, 10 Mexicans, 4 Negroes, 3 South African mixed, 74 South Americans, 9 West Indians). We have counted as Whites the 'Europeans' and South Americans, as Africans the Cubans, Negroes, South Africans and West Indians, as 'Others' the Hawaiians and Mexicans, and as Asiatics all others.

According to *Colonial Report*, 1585, p. 5, 1637, p. 4, 1673, p. 5, 1712, p. 4, 1775, p. 4, *Dominions Office and Colonial Office List, 1937*, p. 320, the civilian population was composed as follows:

	7 March 1931	*30 June 1931*	*30 June 1932*	*30 June 1933*	*30 June 1934*	*30 June 1935*	*30 June 1936*
Non-Chinese	19,369	19,522	19,984	20,446	20,908	21,370	21,832
Chinese ..	821,104	859,425	880,812	902,197	923,584	944,971	966,358

(8) *Report on the Census, 1931*, pp. 41-3, 45-6.

Korea.

(1) 1 October 1930; *Résumé statistique de l'Empire du Japon*, vol. 50, p. 4.

(2) to (5) Ibid., p. 6. These estimates are apparently too low.

(6) 1 October 1935 (Census); ibid., p. 4.

The figures do not include the officers and privates of the Army and Navy residing in Korea; see *Financial and Economic Annual of Japan*, 1935, p. 2.

According to *Résumé*, vol. 50, p. 6, the race distribution was as follows:

	31 Dec. 1931	*31 Dec. 1932*	*31 Dec. 1933*	*31 Dec. 1934*
Japanese	514,666	523,452	543,104	561,384
Natives	19,710,168	20,037,273	20,205,591	20,513,804
Foreigners ..	38,124	39,151	42,626	50,639

'The 1934 returns give the number of British subjects as 188, Americans 696, French 60, and Germans 80' (*Statesman's Year-Book, 1937*, p. 1,107).

Kuria Muria Islands.

(3) to (5) *Year-Book League of Nations, 1933-4* to *1935-6*. According to *Statesman's Year-Book, 1937*, p. 102, 'about 2,200'.

Kwang Chau Wan.

(1) 1 July 1926; *Résultats statistiques du recensement, 1931*, vol. I, part I, p. 113.

(2) to (5) *Year-Book League of Nations, 1932-3* to *1935-6*.

(7) *Résultats statistiques du recensement, 1931*, vol. I, part I, p. 113: (1) Europeans and Assimilated: 266 French, 4 Foreigners; (2) Natives: 206,000.

Kwantung.

(1) 1 October 1930; *Résumé statistique de l'Empire du Japon*, vol. 50, p. 4.

(2) to (5) Ibid., p. 6.

(6) 1 October 1935 (Census); ibid., p. 4.

The figures do not include the officers and privates of the army and navy residing in Kwantung; see *Financial and Economic Annual of Japan, 1935*, p. 2.

According to *Résumé*, vol. 50, p. 6, the race distribution was as follows:

	1 Oct. 1930	*31 Dec. 1931*	*31 Dec. 1932*	*31 Dec. 1933*	*31 Dec. 1934*
Japanese[1] ..	243,559	242,579	272,482	309,029	345,430
Natives (Chinese)	1,081,442	1,030,484	1,049,327	1,097,541	1,149,949
Foreigners ..	3,010	2,122	2,057	2,185	2,221

[1] Including Koreans and Formosans.

Macao.

(1) 31 March 1927; *Anuário do Império Colonial Português, 1935*, p. 3.

(2) to (5) *Year-Book League of Nations, 1932-3* to *1935-6*.

(6) League of Nations, *Annual Epidemiological Report, 1935*, p. 65.

According to *Anuário, 1935*, p. 3: 3,860 Whites; 577 Half-castes; 152,738 Yellows.

According to *Anuário, 1935*, p. 230, many Chinese evaded the 1927 Census, and the population exceeds 275,000 (15 September 1934: 282,035).

Maldive Islands.

(1) 26 February 1931 ; *Colonial Report*, 1797, p. 11.

(3) to (5) *Year-Book League of Nations, 1933-4* to *1935-6*.

(7) *Census Publications, Ceylon, 1921*, vol. I, part II, p. 97. With the exception of 217 foreigners—159 natives of India (137 Boras, 22 'Malabars') and 58 Ceylon Moors—the population was entirely Maldivian.

(8) *Census Publications, Ceylon, 1921*, vol. I, part II, p. 98.

Netherlands Indies.

(1) 7 October 1931 ; *Netherlands Indian Report, 1935, II Statistical Abstract for the Year 1934*, p. 14. Figure excludes the ships' personnel.

(2) to (5) *Year-Book League of Nations, 1932-3* to *1935-6*.

(7) *Statistical Abstract, 1934*, pp. 14-15 : 240,417 'Europeans' (208,269 Netherlanders, 12,899 of Other European Nationalities, 643 Americans, 130 Turks, 542 Armenians, 7,195 Japanese and Formosans, 282 Filipinos, 8,948 Native races, 812 Other Nationalities, 697 Unknown); 59,138,067 Natives ; 1,233,214 Chinese ; 115,535 Other Foreign Asiatics. We have counted as Whites four-fifths of the Netherlanders, Other Europeans, and Americans.

North Borneo.

(1) 26 April 1931 ; *Report on the Census of the State of North Borneo, 1931*, p. 2. Figure includes 254 Sea-going Population.

(2) (4) (6) *Statistical Abstract British Empire, 1925 to 1931*, p. 4; *1924 to 1933*, p. 4; *1926 to 1935*, p. 4.

(3) (5) *Year-Book League of Nations, 1933-4, 1935-6*.

(7) *Census, 1931*, pp. 12-13, 100: 362 Europeans; 236 Eurasians; 47,972 Chinese; 205,218 Natives of Borneo; 11,550 Other Natives of Malay Archipelago ; 4,885 Others (1,298 Natives of India and Ceylon, 7 Siamese, 2,849 Filipinos, 450 Japanese, 244 Arabs, 32 Jews, 2 Africans, 3 Not Stated).

Palestine.

(1) 18 November 1931 ; *Census of Palestine, 1931*, vol. II, p. 2 ; *Report to the Council of the League of Nations on the Administration of Palestine and Trans-Jordan for the Year 1933*, p. 136. Figure includes 2,507 His Majesty's Forces (and families) and 66,553 Nomads.

(2) to (4) *Year-Book League of Nations, 1932-3* to *1934-5*.

(5) (6) Government of Palestine, *Vital Statistics Quarterly Bulletin, 1936*, No. 4, p. 6. Population 31 December 1934-6: 1,144,001, 1,241,561, 1,300,151 'exclusive of Nomads who numbered 66,553 at the Census of 1931, and of Members of His Majesty's Forces.' We have added 66,553 for Nomads.

(7) to (12) *Census, 1931*, vol. I, p. 77; vol. II, pp. 12, 24-5; *Report to League, 1932*, p. 119; *1933*, p. 135; *1934*, p. 139; *Vital Statistics Quarterly Bulletin, 1936*, No. 4, p. 6. On 18 November 1931, there were by 'nationality': 839,619 Arabs; 174,809 Jews; 21,393 Others. The distribution by religion is given as follows:

Date	Moslems	Jews	Christians	Others	Total
18 Nov. 1931	759,712	174,610	91,398	10,101	1,035,821
30 June 1932	704,621	180,793	90,624	10,281	986,319
30 June 1933	723,427	209,207	95,165	10,332	1,038,331
30 June 1934	740,627	253,700	99,532	10,746	1,104,605
31 Dec. 1934	747,824	282,970	102,414	10,793	1,144,001
30 June 1935	759,904	320,358	103,371	10,896	1,194,529
31 Dec. 1935	770,135	355,142	105,243	11,031	1,241,561
30 June 1936	781,789	370,483	106,474	11,219	1,269,965
31 Dec. 1936	796,175	384,085	108,513	11,378	1,300,151

The figure for 18 November 1931 is all-inclusive. All other figures exclude the Nomads and His Majesty's Forces (and families).

The Moslems are nearly all Asiatics. A small proportion of the Jews are Asiatics or Africans. The majority of the Christians are Arabs. The 'Others' are mostly Asiatics. The total number of Whites corresponds probably rather closely to the number of Jews. We have counted all others as Asiatics or Africans, adding the figure of 66,553 for Nomads.

(13) *Census, 1931*, vol. II, pp. 166-7.

Philippines.

(1) 1918; *Statistical Handbook of the Philippine Islands, 1932*, p. vii.

(2) to (6) *Statistical Abstract of the United States, 1936*, p. 10. Figures refer to 30 June. Population, 30 June 1936: 13,269,000.

Portuguese India.

(1) 1931; *Anuário do Império Colonial Português, 1935*, p. 3.

(2) to (5) *Year-Book League of Nations, 1932-3* to *1935-6*.

According to *Anuário, 1935*, p. 3: 1,633 White; 577,786 Hindu; 5 Yellow; 545 Mixed.

Saghalien.

(1) 1 October 1930; *Résumé statistique de l'Empire du Japon*, vol. 50, p. 4.

(2) to (5) Ibid., p. 6.

(6) 1 October 1935 (Census); ibid., p. 4.

The figures do not include the officers and privates of the Army and Navy residing in Saghalien; see *Financial and Economic Annual of Japan, 1935*, p. 2.

According to *Résumé*, vol. 50, p. 6, *Japan Year Book, 1933*, p. 1160, *1935*, p. 1120, *1936*, p. 1126, *Japan Times Year Book, 1933*, p. 297, the race distribution was as follows:

<table>
<tr><th></th><th>1 Oct. 1930</th><th>31 Dec. 1931</th><th>31 Dec. 1932</th><th>31 Dec. 1933</th><th>31 Dec. 1934</th></tr>
<tr><td>Japanese</td><td>284,271</td><td>279,204</td><td rowspan="2">290,950</td><td>293,168</td><td>304,995</td></tr>
<tr><td>Koreans</td><td>8,186[1]</td><td>5,880</td><td>5,043</td><td>5,878</td></tr>
<tr><td>Natives</td><td>2,164</td><td>2,009</td><td>1,937</td><td>1,837</td><td>1,958</td></tr>
<tr><td>Chinese</td><td rowspan="2">575</td><td>90</td><td rowspan="2">285</td><td>59</td><td>72</td></tr>
<tr><td>Other Foreigners</td><td>194[2]</td><td>191[3]</td><td>227[4]</td></tr>
</table>

[1] Including 5 Formosans.
[2] 163 Russians, 28 Poles, 2 Germans, 1 Turk.
[3] 173 Russians, 16 Poles, 2 Germans.
[4] 193 Russians, 26 Poles, 6 Germans, 2 Not stated.

Sarawak.

(2) (4) (5) *Year-Book League of Nations, 1932-3, 1933-4, 1935-6.*

(3) *Statistical Abstract British Empire, 1924 to 1933*, p. 4.

(6) Ibid. *1926 to 1935*, p. 4. According to Sarawak, *Administration Report for 1935*, p. iv: 442,900. 'There are about 390 Europeans in Sarawak' (ibid., p. viii).

Socotra.

(2) to (5) *Year-Book League of Nations, 1932-3* to *1935-6.*

(6) *Dominions Office and Colonial Office List, 1937*, p. 516.

Straits Settlements.

(1) 1 April 1931; British Malaya, *Report on the 1931 Census*, pp. 120-1, 127. Figures include 11,764 'population enumerated on Sea-going Ships', but excludes all persons enumerated on the railway (total for British Malaya, 1,496).

(2) (4) (6) *Statistical Abstract British Empire, 1925 to 1931*, p. 4; *1924 to 1933*, p. 4; *1926 to 1935*, p. 4.

(3) (5) *Year-Book League of Nations, 1933-4, 1935-6.*

Population on 30 June 1932 to 1936: 1,076,564, 1,038,827, 1,057,108, 1,117,023, 1,170,425; see *Colonial Report*, 1655, p. 5; 1682, p. 6; 1726, p. 6; 1783, p. 7; *Dominions Office and Colonial Office List, 1937*, p. 366. In February 1935, the Dindings (population 1931: 19,592) were retroceded to the State of Perak.

(7) *Report on the 1931 Census*, pp. 120-1, 165, 200: 10,003 Europeans (including 710 Dutch, 217 French, and 94 Portuguese, who in part are Half-castes); 11,292 Eurasians; 250,864 Malays (see Brunei); 34,452 other Malaysians; 663,518 Chinese; 132,277 Indians; 11,609 Others (73 Annamese, 2,632 Arabs, 83 Armenians, 2,801 Ceylon Peoples, 381 Filipinos, 3,508 Japanese, 822 Jews, 7 Negroes, 61 Persians, 1,041 Siamese, 200 Others). Figures do not include 11,764 on Sea-going Ships.

According to *Colonial Report*, 1655, p. 5, 1682, p. 6, 1726, p. 6, 1783, p. 7, *Economic Survey of the Colonial Empire (1935)*, p. 186, the distribution by race was as follows:

	30 June 1932	*30 June 1933*	*30 June 1934*	*30 June 1935*	*31 Dec. 1935*
Europeans ..	9,522	9,424	10,275	11,277	12,100
Eurasians ..	11,546	11,550	11,694	11,947	12,048
Malaysians ..	296,465	292,604	296,154	289,617	292,281
Chinese ..	633,436	607,376	617,435	666,626	686,804
Indians ..	114,111	106,502	109,862	125,798	128,821
Others	11,484	11,371	11,688	11,758	11,738

(8) *Report on the 1931 Census*, p. 213. Birthplace of Europeans: Great Britain and Ireland 5,973, Australia 345, New Zealand 72, Canada 32, British Malaya 1,383, Elsewhere in British Empire 515, United States of America 214, Denmark 53, France 178, Germany 100, Holland 383, Netherlands East Indies 195, Elsewhere outside British Empire 540, Not Stated 20. We have counted those born 'elsewhere in British Empire' as born in Asia, and those born 'elsewhere outside British Empire' as born in Europe.

Syria and Lebanon.

(2) to (4) *Year-Book League of Nations, 1932-3* to *1934-5.*

(5) *L'Asie Française, 1935*, p. 160.

(6) *Bulletin de la Statistique générale de la France*, January-March 1937, p. 284. 'A census of the autochthons was taken in Syria in December 1935; in Lebanon the last enumeration of the native population dates from January 1932; finally, the French (citizens, subjects, and protected persons) residing in Syria and in Lebanon

were enumerated in March 1936. It results from these various sources of information that the population of the Levantine States, at the beginning of 1936, was as follows :

		in thousands
Autochthonous population	Lebanon (estimate)	800
	Sandjak of Alexandrette ..	205
	States of the Alawiya ..	350
	State of Jebel Druze ..	64
	Syria (excl. Alexandrette, the Alawiya and Jebel Druze)	1,782
French and assimilated population	.. ..	16
	Total	3,217

The French population was composed as follows: 365 civilian officials with 826 family members; 5,585 officers, non-commissioned officers, and privates, with 3,498 family members; 5,731 other persons (French citizens, subjects or protected persons) not belonging to the preceding classes.'

Timor.

(1) 1931 ; *Anuário do Império Colonial Português, 1935*, p. 3.

(2) to (5) *Year-Book League of Nations, 1932-3* to *1935-6*. For 1934, Hübners *Geographisch-statistische Tabellen, 1936*, p. 282, give 472,220, and *Almanach de Gotha, 1937*, p. 1,222, 463,317.

(6) Census, 15 November 1935 ; Colónia de Moçambique, *Anuário Estatístico, 1935* (quoted from *Notiziario demografico, 1937*, p. 72).

(7) *Anuário do Império, 1935*, p. 3: 625 White; 470,517 Malay; 68 Hindu ; 2,399 Yellow ; 152 Negro ; 602 Mixed.

Trans-Jordan.

(2) (3) (6) *International Yearbook of Agricultural Statistics, 1931-2*, p. 11; *1932-3*, p. 11 ; *1934-5*, p. 11. Figure for 1935 refers to 24 April.

(4) (5) *Report to the Council of the League of Nations on the Administration of Palestine and Trans-Jordan, 1933*, p. 266 ; *1934*, p. 255.

Report, 1935, p. 274, states : 'No census has been taken of the population of Trans-Jordan and any attempt to estimate the number of inhabitants can only be approximate. The total probably lies between 300,000 and 320,000.'

Unfederated Malay States.

(1) 1 April 1931 ; British Malaya, *Report on the 1931 Census*, pp. 120-1, 127. Figures include 563 'population enumerated on

Sea-going Ships', but excludes all persons enumerated on the railway (total for British Malaya 1,496).

(2) (4) (6) *Statistical Abstract British Empire, 1925 to 1931*, p. 4; *1924 to 1933*, p. 4; *1926 to 1935*, p. 4.

(3) (5) *Year-Book League of Nations, 1933-4, 1935-6.*

(7) *Report on the 1931 Census*, pp. 120-1, 201: 1,295 Europeans; 468 Eurasians; 923,912 Malays (see Brunei); 131,941 Other Malaysians; 330,857 Chinese; 110,951 Indians; 27,180 Others (310 Annamese, 1,903 Arabs, 1,982 Ceylon Peoples, 12 Filipinos, 1,597 Japanese, 3 Negroes, 1 Persian, 21,121 Siamese, 251 Others). Figures do not include 563 on Sea-going Ships.

(8) *Report on the 1931 Census*, p. 215. Birthplace of Europeans: Great Britain and Ireland 848, Australia 54, New Zealand 27, British Malaya 186, Elsewhere in British Empire 67, United States of America 8, Denmark 31, France 14, Germany 4, Holland 4, Netherland East Indies 7, Elsewhere outside British Empire 45. We have counted those born 'elsewhere in British Empire' as born in Asia and those born 'elsewhere outside British Empire' as born in Europe.

Europe.

Gibraltar.

(1) 26 April 1931; *The Census of Gibraltar, 1931*, Preface. Figure comprises 17,613 Civil (City 17,405, Port 208); 541 Royal Navy; 3,218 Military.

(2) to (6) *Colonial Report*, 1584, p. 3, 1629, p. 3, 1695, p. 3, 1717, p. 3, 1779, p. 3, give for 31 December 1931 to 1935 as total civil population 16,908, 16,609, 16,397, 15,847 and 16,865 and as fixed civil residents 15,428, 15,143, 15,071, 14,790, and 15,735. 'These figures represent the population between sunset and sunrise, but some 4,500 aliens and 1,500 British subjects resident in the neighbouring Spanish town of La Linea come into Gibraltar daily.' *Gibraltar Blue Book, 1931*, p. 116, *1932*, p. 118, give likewise for 31 December 1931 and 1932, 16,908 and 16,609, but *1933*, p. 128, *1934*, p. 134, *1935*, p. 136, give for 31 December 1933 to 1935, 16,464, 15,987 and 16,992.

(7) *Census, 1931*, Tables IV, XIII. Civil population: 17,494 Europeans, 62 North Africans, 56 East Indians, 1 Chinese.

(8) *Census, 1931*, Tables III, XII.

Malta.

(1) 26 April 1931; *Census of the Maltese Islands, 1931*, p. ii. Figures comprise 241,621 Civilian element, 16,779 Non-civilian element (14,080 Royal Navy, 2,066 Army, 421 Royal Air Force, 50 Royal Fleet Auxiliary Service, 162 Merchant Shipping).

(2) to (6) Malta, *Vital Statistics, April 1932*, p. vi, *Malta Blue Books, 1932-5*, Section 15, p. 4. Population, 31 December 1936: 262,165 (*Vital Statistics, March 1937*, p. vi). Figures comprise Civilian population and families of Military.

(7) *Census, 1931*, pp. 111-12.

Spitzbergen.

(1) 1 December 1930; *Folketellingen i Norge, 1930*, vol. I, p. 27.

(2) to (5) *Year-Book League of Nations, 1932-3* to *1935-6*.

(6) *Almanach de Gotha, 1937*, p. 1171.

OCEANIA.

American Samoa.

(1) 1 April 1930; *Census of the United States, 1930, Outlying Territories and Possessions*, pp. 307, 309: Whites (227) include the naval personnel (178).

(2) (3) (5) *Year-Book League of Nations, 1932-3, 1933-4, 1935-6*.

(4) Hübners *Geographisch-statistische Tabellen, 1936*, p. 314.

(6) *Almanach de Gotha, 1937*, p. 729.

(7) *Census, 1930*, pp. 309, 311: 'The divisions of the population by color or race are: (1) Polynesians, the native race of Samoa; (2) mixed, those of a mixture of Polynesian and any other race; (3) white; and (4) other colored' (6 Japanese, 5 Chinese, 6 Negroes, 8 Others).

(8) *Census, 1930*, pp. 309, 311.

British Solomon Islands.

(1) April 1931; *Colonial Report*, 1790, p. 3.

(2) to (5) *Year-Book League of Nations, 1932-3* to *1935-6*.

(7) *Colonial Report*, 1790, p. 3: 478 Europeans; 89,568 Melanesian Natives; 3,847 Polynesian Natives; 164 Chinese; 8 Japanese; 1 Malay. In April 1935 and 1936, 192 Chinese (see *Dominions Office and Colonial Office List, 1936*, p. 491, *1937*, p. 494).

Caroline, Marianne and Marshall Islands.

(1) 1 October 1930; *Annual Report to the League of Nations on the Administration of the South Sea Islands under Japanese Mandate, 1932*, p. 171.

(2) to (6) *Report to the League, 1931*, p. 140; *1932*, p. 169; *1933*, p. 2; *1934*, p. 80; *1935*, p. 80. Figures refer to 1 October (1935 census figures provisional). The 'figures do not include the number of officers and privates of the army and navy residing there' (*Financial and Economic Annual of Japan, 1935*, p. 2).

(7) to (16) *Report to the League, 1931*, p. 143; *1932*, p. 171; *1933*, p. 4; *1934*, p. 80; *1935*, p. 80; *Financial and Economic Annual, 1935*, p. 2; *Japan-Manchoukuo Year Book, 1937*, p. 568. The race distribution is shown as follows: Japanese (including Koreans and Formosans), Natives, Foreigners. According to *Report to the League, 1930*, p. 132, *1931*, p. 140; *1932*, p. 170, and Paul H. Clyde, *Japan's Pacific Mandate*, p. 149, New York, 1935, the foreigners were of the following nationalities:

	1 Oct. 1930	*1 Oct. 1931*	*1 Oct. 1932*	*1 Oct. 1933*
European	64	70	75	81
American	5	9	4	6
Mexican	—	—	1	—
Colombian	1	1	1	1
Chinese	24	18	14	16
Filipino	1	1	1	—
Australian	1	1	1	—

We have counted the Chinese and the Filipinos as Asiatics and all other foreigners as Whites. For 1 April 1932, 1 April 1933, 1 April 1934, 1 October 1934, 1 April 1935, and 1 October 1935 we have assumed that of the total foreigners (98, 100, 103, 100, 97, 92) five-sixths were Whites and one-sixth Asiatics.

Cook Islands and Niue.

(1) 20 April 1926; Dominion of New Zealand, *Population Census, 1926*, vol. II, p. 1.

(2) to (6) Dominion of New Zealand, *Monthly Abstract of Statistics*, April 1932, p. 1; June 1933, p. 1; April 1934, p. 1; May 1935, p. 1; September 1936, p. 1. Figure for 1933 refers to 30 September. Census, 30 April 1936: 16,350 (ibid., February 1937, p. 1).

According to *Census, 1926*, vol. II, pp. 1-2: '"European" or non-native population' including population 'with less than half

Native blood,' 313; 'Half-castes, i.e. those of half Native blood up to but not including full-blooded Natives,' 562; 'Natives' (full-blooded), 12,988.

Census, 30 April 1936: Non-native population, 277 (*New Zealand Official Year-Book, 1937*, pp. 786-7).

(7) *Census, 1926*, vol. II, p. 2.

Fiji Islands.

(1) 24 April 1921; *Fiji Census, 1921*, p. x.

(2) to (5) *Colonial Report*, 1604, p. 9; 1640, p. 9; 1689, p. 10; 1719, p. 10.

(6) 26 April 1936; *A Report on the Fiji Census, 1936*, p. 4.

(7) *Census, 1921*, pp. 1-3, 176: 3,878 Europeans and other Whites; 2,781 Half-castes (mixture of European and any Native race); 84,475 Fijians; 1,564 Polynesians (immigrants introduced into this Colony under the Polynesian Immigration Ordinance, 1888, and their offspring); 60,634 Indians; 2,235 Rotumans; 910 Chinese; 789 Others: 86 Japanese, 297 Samoans, 108 Tongans, 143 Futuna and Wallis Islanders, 111 Gilbert and Ellice Islanders, 44 Others.

(8) to (12) *Colonial Report*, 1604, p. 9; 1640, p. 9; 1689, p. 10; 1719, p. 10; 1781, p. 10. The race distribution is given as follows:

	31 Dec. 1931	*31 Dec. 1932*	*31 Dec. 1933*	*31 Dec. 1934*	*31 Dec. 1935*
Europeans ..	5,058	4,863	4,804	4,763	4,938
Coloured:					
Half-castes ..	3,446	3,548	3,661	3,717	3,846
Fijians ..	93,414	94,976	96,656	98,479	99,953
Polynesians	1,883	1,889	1,878	1,866	1,982
Indians ..	76,722	78,975	80,991	83,289	85,892
Rotumans ..	2,407	2,457	2,521	2,498	2,561
Chinese ..	1,441	1,460	1,476	1,486	1,486
Others ..	1,202	1,230	1,251	1,351	1,394
Total ..	185,573	189,398	193,238	197,449	202,052

(13) *Census, 1936*, pp. 4-5, 15; *Dominions Office and Colonial Office List, 1937*, p. 292: 4,028 Europeans; 4,574 Half-castes (Anglo-Fijian 3,450, Anglo-Polynesian 711, Others 413); 97,651 Fijians; 3,553 Polynesians (including 2,816 Rotumans); 85,002 Indians; 1,616 Melanesians; 1,751 Chinese; 204 Others (62 Japanese, 125 Gilbert and Ellice Islanders, 1 Caroline Islander, 1 Arab, 7 Negroes, 3 Papuans, 5 Philippine Islanders).

(14) *Census, 1921*, pp. 140-1, 152, 162, 181.

(15) *Census, 1936*, pp. 61-3.

French Settlements.

(1) 1 July 1931; *Bulletin de l'agence générale des colonies May 1932*, p. 825. Figures do not include the population of Rapa (31 December 1935, 266; see *L'Océanie française*, May-July 1936, p. 54), Rimatara and two districts of Tuamotu.

(2) to (5) *Year-Book League of Nations, 1932-3* to *1935-6*.

(7) *Bulletin, May 1932*, p. 826: 5,280 French; 29,101 Oceanians (16,998 French citizens, 11,326 French subjects, 777 Foreigners); 301 English; 122 Other European Nationalities; 169 Americans; 10 Chileans; 10 Syrians; 319 Indo-Chinese; 4,056 Chinese; 37 Japanese; 1 Javanese; 307 floating population. We have counted the Syrians, Indo-Chinese, Chinese, Japanese, and Javanese as Asiatics, the French Oceanians as Natives, the Foreign Oceanians and the floating population as 'Others', and all others as Whites (although many of the 'French' probably are not Whites).

Gilbert and Ellice Islands.

(1) 1931; *Statistical Abstract British Empire, 1926 to 1935*, p. 4.

(2) to (6) *Colonial Report*, 1621, p. 5; 1642, pp. 5-6; 1696, pp. 5-6; 1727, pp. 5-6; 1798, pp. 6-7; *Dominions Office and Colonial Office List, 1936*, p. 489. Figures for 1931 and 1932 refer to 30 June. Figures for 1933-5 exclude Christmas Island (30 June 1932, 33 Natives and 5 Europeans); figures for 1934 and 1935 exclude also Washington Island (31 December 1933, 190 Natives and 4 Europeans), but the Island was uninhabited at the end of 1935 and possibly already at the end of 1934.

(7) Gilbert and Ellice Islands Colony, *Blue Book for the Year from 1st April 1934 to 31st March 1935*, p. 44: 249 Europeans; 28,496 Micronesians; 3,668 Polynesians; 728 Chinese; 231 Others.

(8) *Colonial Report*, 1621, p. 5: 'Micronesians 28,275, Polynesians 4,183, Mongolians 439, Europeans 275, half-castes 235, Melanesians 5, and others 4.'

(9) to (12) *Colonial Report*, 1642, p. 5; 1696, p. 5; 1727, p. 5; 1798, p. 6. Population subdivided into Europeans, Asiatics, and Natives.

Guam.

(1) 1 April 1930; *Census of the United States, 1930, Outlying Territories and Possessions*, p. 289. 'Includes population (1,118) of United States naval reservations, and persons on the United States ships stationed at Guam.'

(2) (4) *Year-Book League of Nations, 1932-3, 1934-5*.

(3) 30 June 1932; *International Yearbook of Agricultural Statistics, 1934-5*, p. 17.

(5) Hübners *Geographisch-statistische Tabellen, 1936*, p. 314.

(6) 30 June 1935; *Statesman's Year-Book, 1936*, p. 652.

(7) *Census, 1930*, pp. 291-2: 16,402 Chamorros (the Native inhabitants, 'a hybrid race, being a mixture of Malayan, Spanish, Mexican, English, and other races, with the Malayan strain predominating'); 1,205 Whites; 365 Filipinos; 297 Japanese; 203 Chinese; 37 Negroes. Whites include 892 naval population.

According to *Statesman's Year-Book, 1937*, p. 660, 20,047 of the 21,496 inhabitants on 30 June 1936 were classed as Natives.

(8) *Census, 1930*, pp. 291-2.

Hawaii.

(1) 1 April 1930; *Census of the United States, 1930, Outlying Territories and Possessions*, p. 41.

(2) United States Department of the Interior, *Annual Report of the Governor of Hawaii, 1931-2*, p. 103.

(3) to (5) *Year-Book League of Nations, 1933-4* to *1935-6*.

(6) 30 June 1935; *Annual Report, 1934-5*, p. 34. Population, 30 June 1936 (ibid., *1935-6*, p. 31): 393,277.

The population on 30 June 1931 to 1934 was according to *Annual Report, 1930-1*, p. 45; *1931-2*, p. 103; *1932-3*, p. 22; *1933-4*, p. 33: 375,211, 380,507, 380,211, and 378,948.

(7) to (13) *Census, 1930*, pp. 45, 48; *Annual Report, 1930-1*, p. 45; *1931-2*, p. 103; *1933-4*, p. 33; *1934-5*, p. 34; *1935-6*, p. 31:

Racial Classification	*1 April 1930*	*30 June 1931*	*31 Dec. 1931*	*30 June 1932*	*30 June 1934*	*30 June 1935*	*30 June 1936*
Hawaiian[1]	22,636	22,391	22,310	22,230	21,796	21,710	21,594
Caucasian-Hawaiian[2]	15,632	16,454	16,755	17,056	18,169	18,742	19,391
Asiatic-Hawaiian[3]	12,592	13,549	14,004	14,459	16,250	17,236	18,217
Portuguese	27,588	28,219	28,407	28,595	29,236	29,550	29,863
Puerto Rican	6,671	6,886	6,943	7,000	7,280	7,368	7,470
Spanish	1,219	1,255	1,254	1,253	1,267	1,267	1,261
Other Caucasian[4]	44,895	41,968	42,743	43,517	45,888	50,258	57,069
Chinese	27,179	27,317	27,276	27,235	26,989	27,264	27,495
Japanese	139,631	143,754	144,972	146,189	148,024	148,972	149,886
Korean	6,461	6,583	6,618	6,653	6,638	6,668	6,682
Filipino	63,052	66,049	65,782	65,515	56,700	54,668	53,550
Others	780[5]	786	795	805	711	754	799

1 Pure Hawaiians.

2 Mixture of Caucasian and Hawaiian stock.

3 Mixture of Asiatic and Hawaiian stock. 'About one-third of the Asiatic-Hawaiians also have Caucasian blood' (Frederick V. Field, *Economic Handbook of the Pacific Area*, p. 48, New York, 1934).

4 'Includes a military population of about 20,000' (Field, p. 47).

5 563 Negroes; 217 Other Races.

The 'Caucasians' (Portuguese, Puerto Rican, Spanish, Other Caucasian) doubtless include Half-castes. We have counted as Whites the Portuguese, the Spanish, and the other Caucasians.

(14) *Census, 1930*, pp. 63-4.

Nauru.

(1) 24 April 1921; *Census of Nauru, 1921.*

(2) to (6) Administration of Nauru, *Annual Census, 1st April 1936.* Figures for 1931, 1932, 1934 and 1935 refer to 1 April, figure for 1933 to 30 June (Census). Population 1 April 1936, 2,922.

(7) to (12) *Annual Census, 1st April 1936.* The population is subdivided into Europeans, Chinese (Indentured labourers), Nauruans and other Pacific Islanders.

(13) to (16) *Census of the Commonwealth of Australia, 30th June 1933, Census Bulletin,* No. 7, pp. 3, 5-6; Administration of Nauru, *Annual Census, 1st April 1934; Government Gazette,* 21 September 1935; *Annual Census, 1st April 1936.*

New Caledonia.

(1) 1 July 1931; *Bulletin de l'agence générale des colonies,* December 1932, p. 1871.

(2) to (5) *Year-Book League of Nations, 1932-3* to *1935-6.*

(6) 1 July 1936; *L'Océanie Française,* January-February 1937, p. 15.

(7) *Bulletin,* December 1932, pp. 1,871-6; *L'Océanie Française,* November-December 1931, p. 111: 15,165 French (3,042 born in France, 10,703 born in the Colony, 623 penal population, 282 troops, 515 commercial ship crews in harbours); 2,050 free Foreigners; 11,448 indentured Immigrants (6,198 Javanese, 5,026 Tonkinese, 164 New-Hebrideans, 40 Indians, 20 Wallis Islanders); 28,502 Natives. There were in addition 111 Natives at the Colonial Exhibition in Paris. The free foreigners include many Japanese (1 July 1921: 1,751; 1 July 1933: 1,100; see *L'Océanie Française,* May-June 1934, p. 47). We have counted one-third of the free foreigners as Whites and two-thirds as Asiatics.

For some sections of the population figures have been published for intercensal years:

Indentured Javanese, 31 December 1931, 5,372; 1 December 1932, 4,823; 1934, 3,544. Indentured Indo-Chinese, 31 December 1931, 3,199; 1 December 1932, 1,604; 1934, 2,345. Free residents controlled by the Labour Office, 1934, 796 (696 Javanese, 100 Annamese). See *L'Océanie Française,* November-December 1934, pp. 120-1.

Natives, 1932, 27,900; 30 September 1933, 28,043; 1934, 28,275; 1935, 28,229; 1936, 28,596. See *L'Océanie Française,* January-February 1934, p. 20; November-December 1935, p. 116; November-December 1936, p. 97; *Revue d'histoire des colonies, 1935, Memento Colonial,* p. 5.

(8) *L'Océanie Française*, January-February 1937, p. 15: 17,384 'White population' (including 329 penal population and the free Asiatics); 7,061 coloured (indentured) immigrants; 28,800 Natives. We have counted 95 per cent. of the 'White population' as Whites and 5 per cent. as Asiatics.

All figures for New Caledonia apparently exclude the Wallis Archipelago, Futuna, and Alofi with a combined population of 5,972 on 1 July 1931 (*Almanach de Gotha, 1937* p. 1,052) and of 6,492 on 31 December 1935 (*Colonies Autonomes*, September-December 1936, p. 17).

New Guinea.

(2) to (6) Commonwealth of Australia, *Report to the Council of the League of Nations on the Administration of the Territory of New Guinea, 1931-2*, p. 96; *1933-4*, p. 104; *1934-5*, p. 98; *Official Year Book of the Commonwealth of Australia, 1932*, p. 457; *1933*, p. 356; *1934*, p. 364; *1935*, p. 868; *1936*, p. 378.

The non-native population has been enumerated or estimated for the whole Mandated Territory for 30 June 1931-6 as follows: 4,142, 4,366, 5,216, 5,453, 5,688, and 5,881. See *Report, 1931-2*, p. 96; *1933-4*, p. 104; *1934-5*, p. 98; *Dominions Office and Colonial Office List, 1937*, p. 92. The enumerated native population on 30 June 1929-36 was as follows: 370,166, 400,135, 392,816, 389,931, 401,129, 456,924, 478,686, and 500,040. See *Report, 1928-9*, pp. 16, 115; *1929-30*, p. 137; *1930-1*, p. 20; *1931-2*, p. 20; *1932-3*, p. 33; *1933-4*, p. 31; *1934-5*, pp. 103-4; *Dominions Office and Colonial Office List, 1937*, p. 92. The apparent decrease from 1930 to 1932 is attributed to closer enumeration: 'The decrease in the total number of the recorded population of the Territory is due largely to a revision of the figures in the light of the more accurate information obtained from the census and not to any actual decrease of population, except in the District of New Ireland (*Report, 1930-1*, p. 20). 'The calculation of the native population at 30th June 1931, had been made before the census was complete, and was subject to such alteration as was found necessary when the figures were finally reviewed' (*Report, 1931-2*, p. 20). The apparent increase from 1932 to 1935 was largely due to closer enumeration and to the extension of the area under Government control or influence; see, for example, *Report, 1934-5*, p. 26: 'Increases throughout the Territory are due mainly to the enumeration of population in newly-opened areas, and to additional names being recorded in areas under control and influence.'

'Only those natives whose names were actually noted during the course of patrols have been reckoned in the count of the population, and the number mentioned does not therefore include natives who were living beyond the sphere of Government influence' (*Report, 1931-2*, p. 20). The earlier Reports to the League contained estimates of the 'population of areas patrolled but not under complete control'; for example, 30 June 1929: 117,100; 30 June 1930: 121,250 (see *Report, 1928-9*, p. 115; *1929-30*, p. 137). But the *Report, 1930-1*, p. 120, stated: 'Statistics for previous years included an estimate of the population of areas patrolled but not under complete control. Owing to the inadequacy of the data the preparation of such an estimate has been discontinued.' There are in addition vast areas which have not been patrolled. Of 93,000 sq. m. only 38,565 sq. m. were under Government control or influence or penetrated by patrols on 30 June 1930, and 52,746 sq. m. on 30 June 1934 (see *Report, 1929-30*, p. 101; *1933-4*, p. 24).

According to *Official Year Book of the Commonwealth of Australia, 1932*, p. 457, *1933*, p. 356, *1934*, p. 364, *1935*, p. 868, *1936*, p. 378, the total native population was 'estimated roughly' for 30 June 1931 and 1932 at 'about 520,000' (excluding 27,765 and 26,606 indentured labourers) and for 30 June 1933, 1934, and 1935 at 'about 666,000' (including 28,242, 30,595, and 33,993 indentured labourers). This would imply a non-enumerated native population of about 155,000, 157,000, 265,000, 209,000, and 187,000. In *Statesman's Year-Book, 1935*, p. 444, the non-enumerated native population was estimated for 30 June 1934 at 250,000.

(7) (8) *Census of Australia, 1933, Bulletin*, No. 6, p. 8. Non-Indigenous population:

	4 April 1921		*30 June 1933*	
	Full-blood	*Half-caste*	*Full-blood*	*Half-caste*
European	1,288	—	3,191	—
Chinese	1,424	2	1,449	—
Filipino	45	6	57	7
Native of India	1	—	—	—
Japanese	87	2	73	—
Javanese	43	4	61	—
Malay	178	1	132	1
Maori	—	—	—	1
Papuan	—	—	—	8
Polynesian (other)	28	54	42	178
Timorese	2	—	11	—
Other and Indefinite ..	8	—	5	—
Total	3,104	69	5,021	195

(9) (10) *Census of Australia, 1933, Bulletin*, No. 6, p. 6.

New Hebrides (Condominium).

(2) to (5) *Year-Book League of Nations, 1932-3* to *1935-6*.

The non-native population numbered in 1931-5: 4,534, 2,993, 2,318, 2,301 and 1,902 respectively; see *Colonial Report*, 1600, p. 5; 1643, p. 5; 1681, p. 5; 1752, p. 5; 1786, p. 5. The native population has never been enumerated. 'The primitive state of the New Hebrides precludes the taking of any reliable census of the indigenous population. In certain islands which have been under missionary influence for a number of years it is possible to make a fairly accurate estimate of the inhabitants, but in the more uncivilized islands such as Malekula, Pentecost, and Santo, whose interiors are almost a closed book, it is not possible to form more than a rough estimate of their numbers.' (*Colonial Report*, 1786, p. 6.) The total number of natives has been given for a number of years in *Colonial Reports* as 'some 40,000-60,000', in the *Statistical Abstract British Empire* as 50,000; *Dominions Office and Colonial Office List, 1936*, Table following p. xc, gives 47,500; *Résultats statistiques du recensement, 1931*, vol. I, part I, p. 113, gave for 1929: 59,000; *Colonies Autonomes*, September 1935, p. 123, give 'about 40,000'; *Almanach de Gotha, 1937*, p. 1,054, gives for 1936: 43,000.

(7) to (11) *Colonial Report*, 1600, p. 5; 1643, p. 5; 1681, p. 5; 1752, p. 5; 1786, p. 5. Non-Natives:

Year	*Nationals*		*Foreigners opted under Protocol*		*Asiatics opted under Protocol*		*Protected Subjects and Citizens (French)*	
	British	*French*	*British*	*French*	*British*	*French*	*Tonkinese*	*Javanese*
1931 ..	227	791	20	45	30	35	3,344[1]	42
1932 ..	214	789	20	45	36	34	1,813	42
1933 ..	180	789	18	32	42	29	1,166	62
1934 ..	202	731	14	32	54	86	1,181	1
1935 ..	178	731	12	32	61	64	822	2

[1] Includes 44 Chinese.

The Asiatics opted under Protocol consisted in 1933 of 42 Chinese and 29 Japanese, in 1934 of 106 Chinese and 34 Japanese, in 1935 of 93 Chinese and 32 Japanese.

Norfolk.

(1) 4 April 1921; *Census of the Commonwealth of Australia, 30th June 1933, Bulletin*, No. 8, p. 5.

(2) (3) (5) (6) *Official Year Book of the Commonwealth of Australia, 1932*, p. 448; *1933*, p. 347; *1935*, p. 858; *1936*, p. 368. Figures refer to 30 June. Population, 30 June 1936, 1,142 (*Dominions Office and Colonial Office List, 1937*, p. 89).

(4) 30 June 1933; *Census of Australia, 1933, Bulletin*, No. 8, p. 5.

(7) *Census of Australia, 1933, Bulletin*, No. 8, p. 6 : 713 Europeans, 3 Negro half-castes, 1 Polynesian half-caste.

(8) Ibid., p. 6 : 1,230 Europeans, 1 Polynesian half-caste.

(9) (10) Ibid., p. 5.

Papua.

(2) to (5) *Year-Book League of Nations, 1932-3* to *1935-6*.

(6) *Statistical Abstract British Empire, 1926 to 1935*, p. 4.

The European population on 30 June 1931 to 1936 was : 1,128, 1,152, 1,148, 1,107, 1,229, and 1,203 ; see Commonwealth of Australia, *Territory of Papua, Annual Report for the Year 1931-2*, p. 25 ; *1933-4*, p. 31 ; *1934-5*, p. 38 ; *Statesman's Year-Book 1937*, p. 430. There were in addition on 30 June 1933, 1,025 non-European non-Natives.

'A census of a portion of the indigenous population has been taken and the total number of natives actually counted is 224,908, chiefly residing on the coasts. In the past the total population had been estimated at 275,000 but the expedition of Messrs. Hides and O'Malley from the Strickland River to the Perrari River in the first half of 1935 revealed a large population in that tract of country hitherto unknown. Until further investigations of that area are made it is impossible to estimate the additional population discovered.' (*Dominions Office and Colonial Office List, 1937*, p. 86.)

(7) (8) *Census of Australia, 1933, Bulletin*, No. 5, p. 8. Non-Indigenous Population :

	4 April 1921		*30 June 1933*[1]	
	Full-blood	*Half-caste*	*Full-blood*	*Half-caste*
European	1,343	—	1,148	—
Australian (Aboriginal) ..	—	1	—	7
Chinese	3	—	5	—
Cingalese	7	—	4	—
Fijian	85	—	57	—
Filipino	91	2	88	1
Native of India	14	—	16	—
Japanese	10	—	14	—
Javanese	11	—	3	—
Malay	63	—	158	1
Negro	5	—	9	—
Papuan	—	152	—	212
Polynesian (other) ..	287	3	431	6
Other	1	—	1	—
Total	1,920	158	1,934	227

[1] In addition, 12 Not Stated.

(9) (10) *Census of Australia, 1933, Bulletin*, No. 5, p. 6.

Tokelau Islands.

(1) February 1926; Dominion of New Zealand, *Population Census, 1926*, vol. II, p. 5.

(2) (4) (5) (6) Dominion of New Zealand, *Monthly Abstract of Statistics*, June 1933, p. 1; July 1934, p. 1; August 1935, p. 1; December 1936, p. 1. Figures refer to August 1931, June 1933, June 1934 and August 1935. Census, 4 November 1936, 1,170 (ibid., February 1937, p. 1).

(7) *Population Census, 1926*, vol. II, p. 5: 'No Europeans reside in the islands at the present time, and visits from them are very infrequent.' Half-castes numbered 25.

Tonga.

(1) 27 April 1931; *Tonga Government Gazette*, 3 March 1932, p. 24.

(2) (6) *Statistical Abstract British Empire, 1925 to 1931*, p. 4; *1926 to 1935*, p. 4.

(3) 27 April 1932; *Tonga Government Gazette*, 27 March 1933, p. 20.

(4) 27 April 1933; *Colonial Report*, 1701, p. 5.

(5) 27 April 1934; *Colonial Report*, 1724, p. 5.

(7) to (11) *Colonial Report*, 1612, p. 5; 1638, p. 5; 1701, p. 5; 1724, p. 5; 1787, p. 5. For 31 December 1931, see A. H. Wood, *History and Geography of Tonga*, p. 90, Nuku' Alofa, 1932.

The race distribution is given as follows:

Race	*27 April 1931*	*31 Dec. 1931*	*27 April 1932*	*27 April 1933*	*27 April 1934*	*27 April 1935*
Tongans	27,700	29,157	28,381	29,620	30,482	30,724
Europeans	482	...	412	409	378	434
Half-castes	265	...	397	436	475	352
Other Pacific Islanders	336	...	222	185	206	229
Others	56	...	42	43	48	134
Total	28,839	...	29,454	30,693	31,589	31,873

According to Wood (pp. 90-1), 'a considerable proportion of those officially classed as "full-blooded Tongans" have some admixture of foreign blood (mostly European)'. The Asiatics (included among 'Others') 'are mostly Japanese storekeepers and Indian tailors, saddlers and house-servants'.

Western Samoa.

(1) 1 January 1926; Dominion of New Zealand, *Population Census, 1926*, vol. II, p. 6.

(2) to (6) Dominion of New Zealand, *Monthly Abstract of Statistics*, April 1932, p. 1; July 1933, p. 1; June 1934, p. 1; April 1935, p. 1; April 1936, p. 1. The figures for 1931, 1932, and 1933 were derived from the 1926 census by adding the excess of births over deaths and the excess of arrivals over departures. But a count taken during the yaws campaign in 1932-3 yielded for 31 December 1932 and 1933 a population of 47,819 and 52,199 respectively. (See *Report of the Government of New Zealand on the Administration of the Mandated Territory of Western Samoa, 1932-3*, p. 18; *1933-4*, p. 20. See also Dr. S. M. Lambert, 'Annual Report on Western Pacific Health Service,' 1932 and 1933, in Fiji, *Annual Medical Report, 1932*, p. 38; *1933*, p. 41.) The figures for 1934 and 1935 are derived from the latter figure by adding the excess of births over deaths and the excess of arrivals over departures. Census, 4 November 1936, 55,946 (*Monthly Abstract*, February 1937, p. 1).

According to *Census, 1926*, vol. II, pp. 6-8: 'Europeans, including Half-castes with more than one-half European blood, 907; Native Samoans, 36,880; Half-castes with one-half or less European blood, 1,363 (including 94 with Chinese blood); Chinese, 924; Melanesian contract labourers, 155.

The *Reports on the Administration of the Mandated Territory* (*1932-3*, p. 18; *1933-4*, p. 20; *1934-5*, p. 23; *1935-6*, p. 25) contain the following data:

	1 Jan. 1932	*31 Dec. 1932*	*31 Dec. 1933*	*31 Dec. 1934*	*31 Mar. 1936*
Europeans	614	612	601	592	596
Persons of European and Samoan descent . .	2,269	2,323	2,381	2,396	2,447
Native Samoans	42,296	44,126	48,486	49,501	51,094
Chinese labourers	714	638	632	503	503
Melanesian labourers . .	130	120	99	95	93
Total	46,023	47,819	52,199	53,087	54,733

The 'Europeans' probably comprise all persons with more than one-half European blood; the 'Persons of European and Samoan descent' probably include also Half-castes of Chinese descent.

(7) *Population Census, 1926*, vol. II, pp. 7, 9. 'Europeans' include Half-castes with more than one-half European blood and also 34 free Chinese citizens. Nationality of the 'Europeans': 538 British, 294 other European, 81 American, 20 Chinese, 8 Not Stated.

INDEX